Social Credit: Nightmare on Your Street

What social credit means for you, and how it will change your life forever.

Vernon Coleman

Vernon Coleman: What the papers say

'Vernon Coleman writes brilliant books.' – The Good Book Guide
'No thinking person can ignore him.' – The Ecologist
'The calmest voice of reason.' – The Observer
'A godsend.' – Daily Telegraph
'Superstar.' – Independent on Sunday
'Brilliant!' – The People
'Compulsive reading.' – The Guardian
'His message is important.' – The Economist
'He's the Lone Ranger, Robin Hood and the Equalizer rolled into one.' – Glasgow Evening Times
'The man is a national treasure.' – What Doctors Don't Tell You
'His advice is optimistic and enthusiastic.' – British Medical Journal
'Revered guru of medicine.' – Nursing Times
'Gentle, kind and caring' – Western Daily Press
'His trademark is that he doesn't mince words. Far funnier than the usual tone of soupy piety you get from his colleagues.' – The Guardian
'Dr Coleman is one of our most enlightened, trenchant and sensitive dispensers of medical advice.' – The Observer
'I would much rather spend an evening in his company than be trapped for five minutes in a radio commentary box with Mr Geoffrey Boycott.' – Peter Tinniswood, Punch
'Hard hitting...inimitably forthright.' – Hull Daily Mail
'Refreshingly forthright.' – Liverpool Daily Post
'Outspoken and alert.' – Sunday Express
'Dr Coleman made me think again.' – BBC World Service
'Marvellously succinct, refreshingly sensible.' – The Spectator
'Probably one of the most brilliant men alive today.' – Irish Times
'King of the media docs.' – The Independent
'Britain's leading medical author.' – The Star
'Britain's leading health care campaigner.' – The Sun
'Perhaps the best known health writer for the general public in the world today.' – The Therapist
'The patient's champion.' – Birmingham Post

'A persuasive writer whose arguments, based on research and experience, are sound.' – Nursing Standard
'The doctor who dares to speak his mind.' – Oxford Mail
'He writes lucidly and wittily.' – Good Housekeeping

Books by Vernon Coleman include:

Medical
The Medicine Men
Paper Doctors
Everything You Want To Know About Ageing
The Home Pharmacy
Aspirin or Ambulance
Face Values
Stress and Your Stomach
A Guide to Child Health
Guilt
The Good Medicine Guide
An A to Z of Women's Problems
Bodypower
Bodysense
Taking Care of Your Skin
Life without Tranquillisers
High Blood Pressure
Diabetes
Arthritis
Eczema and Dermatitis
The Story of Medicine
Natural Pain Control
Mindpower
Addicts and Addictions
Dr Vernon Coleman's Guide to Alternative Medicine
Stress Management Techniques
Overcoming Stress
The Health Scandal
The 20 Minute Health Check
Sex for Everyone
Mind over Body
Eat Green Lose Weight
Why Doctors Do More Harm Than Good
The Drugs Myth

Complete Guide to Sex
How to Conquer Backache
How to Conquer Pain
Betrayal of Trust
Know Your Drugs
Food for Thought
The Traditional Home Doctor
Relief from IBS
The Parent's Handbook
Men in Bras, Panties and Dresses
Power over Cancer
How to Conquer Arthritis
How to Stop Your Doctor Killing You
Superbody
Stomach Problems – Relief at Last
How to Overcome Guilt
How to Live Longer
Coleman's Laws
Millions of Alzheimer Patients Have Been Misdiagnosed
Climbing Trees at 112
Is Your Health Written in the Stars?
The Kick-Ass A–Z for over 60s
Briefs Encounter
The Benzos Story
Dementia Myth

Psychology/Sociology
Stress Control
How to Overcome Toxic Stress
Know Yourself (1988)
Stress and Relaxation
People Watching
Spiritpower
Toxic Stress
I Hope Your Penis Shrivels Up
Oral Sex: Bad Taste and Hard To Swallow
Other People's Problems

The 100 Sexiest, Craziest, Most Outrageous Agony Column Questions (and Answers) Of All Time
How to Relax and Overcome Stress
Too Sexy To Print
Psychiatry
Are You Living With a Psychopath?

Politics and General
England Our England
Rogue Nation
Confronting the Global Bully
Saving England
Why Everything Is Going To Get Worse Before It Gets Better
The Truth They Won't Tell You...About The EU
Living In a Fascist Country
How to Protect & Preserve Your Freedom, Identity & Privacy
Oil Apocalypse
Gordon is a Moron
The OFPIS File
What Happens Next?
Bloodless Revolution
2020
Stuffed
The Shocking History of the EU
Coming Apocalypse
Covid-19: The Greatest Hoax in History
Old Man in a Chair
Endgame
Proof that Masks do more harm than Good
Covid-19: The Fraud Continues
Covid-19: Exposing the Lies

Diaries and Autobiography
Diary of a Disgruntled Man
Just another Bloody Year
Bugger off and Leave Me Alone
Return of the Disgruntled Man
Life on the Edge

The Game's Afoot
Tickety Tonk
Memories 1
Memories 2

Animals
Why Animal Experiments Must Stop
Fighting For Animals
Alice and Other Friends
Animal Rights – Human Wrongs
Animal Experiments – Simple Truths

General Non Fiction
How to Publish Your Own Book
How to Make Money While Watching TV
Strange but True
Daily Inspirations
Why Is Public Hair Curly
People Push Bottles Up Peaceniks
Secrets of Paris
Moneypower
101 Things I Have Learned
100 Greatest Englishmen and Englishwomen
Cheese Rolling, Shin Kicking and Ugly Tattoos
One Thing after Another

Novels (General)
Mrs Caldicot's Cabbage War
Mrs Caldicot's Knickerbocker Glory
Mrs Caldicot's Oyster Parade
Mrs Caldicot's Turkish Delight
Deadline
Second Chance
Tunnel
Mr Henry Mulligan
The Truth Kills
Revolt
My Secret Years with Elvis

Balancing the Books
Doctor in Paris
Stories with a Twist in the Tale (short stories)
Dr Bullock's Annals

The Young Country Doctor Series
Bilbury Chronicles
Bilbury Grange
Bilbury Revels
Bilbury Country
Bilbury Village
Bilbury Pie (short stories)
Bilbury Pudding (short stories)
Bilbury Tonic
Bilbury Relish
Bilbury Mixture
Bilbury Delights
Bilbury Joys
Bilbury Tales
Bilbury Days
Bilbury Memories

Novels (Sport)
Thomas Winsden's Cricketing Almanack
Diary of a Cricket Lover
The Village Cricket Tour
The Man Who Inherited a Golf Course
Around the Wicket
Too Many Clubs and Not Enough Balls

Cat books
Alice's Diary
Alice's Adventures
We Love Cats
Cats Own Annual
The Secret Lives of Cats
Cat Basket
The Cataholics' Handbook

Cat Fables
Cat Tales
Catoons from Catland

As Edward Vernon
Practice Makes Perfect
Practise What You Preach
Getting Into Practice
Aphrodisiacs – An Owner's Manual
The Complete Guide to Life

Written with Donna Antoinette Coleman
How to Conquer Health Problems between Ages 50 & 120
Health Secrets Doctors Share With Their Families
Animal Miscellany
England's Glory
Wisdom of Animals

Copyright Vernon Coleman June 2022
The right of Vernon Coleman to be identified as the author of this work has been asserted in accordance with the Copyright, Designs and Patents Act 1988.

Dedicated to Antoinette
Always and all ways
All my love will always be all yours.

Note 1
The people behind the Great Reset like to try to demean the truth-tellers by calling us 'conspiracy theorists' and so it is entirely appropriate that we refer to them as the conspirators. What they are doing is no theoretical exercise – it is cruel, practical reality.

Since early summer 2020, I have referred to the people who are supporting the conspirators as the collaborators. The collaborators include the journalists and broadcasters who took money from the conspirators for telling lies on their behalf, the doctors who gave the covid jabs, the teachers who closed schools when closing schools was never necessary, the police who arrested citizens for having picnics in parks and the authorities who, during the lockdowns in the UK, fined a student £10,000 for organising a snowball fight and fined a beggar £434 for holding out his cap at King's Cross railway station in London but fined the Prime Minister, Boris Johnson (who had authorised the lockdowns) a considerably more modest £50 for attending one party and nothing whatsoever for attending another.

Note 2
Throughout this book the word 'man' is used to denote a human of either, or indeed any, sex whether genetic or chosen. Similarly, the word 'men' is used to denote a group of humans of either, or any, sex whether genetic or chosen. This is done merely to avoid unnecessary clumsiness and not to cause anguish. I mention this in a, probably ineffective, attempt to deflect criticism from aggressive feminists who might otherwise be tempted to slam the book with a one star review in a petty response to something that they might wrongly regard as sexist terminology. I should also mention that various changes have been made to the terminology used in this book so as to avoid upsetting the censors too much. (In the past two years four of my books have been banned.) So, for example, the word 'plague' occasionally appears in the book, as does the phrase 'the rebranded flu' – an occasionally necessary alternative name for a disease which ends in a number larger than 18 and smaller than 20. And a four letter word commonly used to describe an item worn by the Lone Ranger and assorted bank robbers is replaced here with the

phrase 'face covering'. All this may seem odd but other people are allowed to use words which I am not allowed to use. (If you want to know more about the ways in which I am constrained, please read the Appendix at the back of this book.)

Contents

Foreword
Part One
What is Social Credit? What does it mean? How does it work?
Part Two
How will Social Credit change your life?
Part Three
So, what do we do?
Appendix
The Author's Travails

Foreword

Most people in the so-called developed world (a phrase which becomes more absurd as the days speed by) have probably heard of 'social credit', but I doubt if one in a hundred understand exactly what it means, what the implications are and precisely how social credit fits into the Great Reset.

It is no exaggeration to say that social credit and the Great Reset, as promoted by the members and partners of the World Economic Forum together with the United Nations, the World Health Organisation and a bunch of independent, unelected billionaires, are leading us into a world in which our every move, deed and, indeed, thought, will be dominated by the evil principles of constant surveillance and control.

It is social credit which will lead us straight into the sort of world predicted by Orwell in 1984 and envisaged by Huxley in Brave New World. Under the control of the New World Order, your body, your mind, your spirit and everything you once thought you owned will belong to the conspirators and their world state. Social credit is the finale. Once it is here, we are fixed firmly in the Great Reset. Life as we knew it will have disappeared forever. We will all live in an upside-down, inside-out world seemingly created by M.C.Escher. We will inhabit a nightmare, alien place far more inhuman than anything envisaged by Jacque Tati. We will all be expected to constrain our ambitions, avoid all controversy and suppress all our original ideas.

It sometimes seems as though things are happening very quickly – and as though new problems are coming at us so quickly that everything is out of control.

In fact, everything is under control.

I've been warning for some time that the bad things that have been happening, are happening and are going to get worse, much worse, were planned a long time ago.

There is plenty of evidence for the fact that clear plans for the Great Reset and the New World Order were already in place back in the 1960s.

Consider, for example, what Dr Richard Day, a professor of paediatrics, had to say in a speech to the Pittsburgh Pediatric Society in the US in 1969. The title of the speech was 'A New World System' and I don't know whether he was trying to warn people or unburden himself but his warnings and predictions were extraordinarily accurate.

Dr Day warned that in the future the elderly would be eliminated by making it more difficult for them to access medical care. He warned that social chaos would be promoted, that travel would be restricted, that hospitals would become jails, that private medicine would be eliminated, that the incidence of heart attacks would be deliberately increased, that the world population would be reduced, that information would be controlled, that fake science would be used to promote the myth of global warming, that there would be cameras everywhere, that sport would become unisex and that ID cards would be implanted. He warned that food supplies would be controlled, that the weather would be controlled and that people would be controlled. ('Control food, control people,' said Henry Kissinger.)

He also warned that books would be banned and removed from libraries if they were considered 'dangerous'. (Many of my books have been banned. My websites are suppressed and regularly hacked and I've been banned from every social media outlet I know of.)

Professor Day warned that television sets would be able to watch the people who were watching them, that cancer cures were being suppressed as a means of population control and that new diseases would be deliberately introduced.

(I reckon the first of these new diseases was AIDS – back in the 1980s. My criticism of the way governments and the media exaggerated the fear to create false terror about AIDS resulted in my being banned by mainstream television and radio – especially the BBC – simply because I produced facts which proved they were lying. They don't like facts, of course. Back in the 80s we were warned that everyone would be affected by AIDS by the year 2000. Medical organisations were constantly producing unsubstantiated scare stories. In 1988, a big publishing house in London suddenly abandoned a big publicity campaign for a book of mine when it was pointed out to them that the short chapter on AIDS didn't fit the Government's plan.)

Dr Day clearly knew what he was talking about because everything he warned about has already come about.

The plague fraud, the global warming fraud, the digital vaccine passport and the manufactured war in Ukraine were all designed and executed to lead us somewhere – to social credit and the Great Reset talked about with such enthusiasm by the rabid lunatics at the World Economic Forum. The deliberately created chaos caused fear and depression and these led easily to compliance – preparing the way for the introduction of a full menu of social credit applications and requirements.

Social credit is the finishing line of this marathon of abuse and deceit.

A few years ago, in a book called 'The Game's Afoot' (published in 2018) I wrote that the Chinese Government was giving people marks according to behaviour. It was, I wrote, called social engineering, and citizens were being ranked and rated according to their behaviour.

'The Government,' I said, 'will measure people's behaviour in order to decide what services they are entitled to. Anyone who incurs black marks for traffic offences, fare dodging or jay working will find that they are no longer entitled to the full range of public services and rights. Moreover, internet activity will also be used to assess behaviour. Individuals who do 'bad' things on the internet, or whose searches are considered questionable, will find themselves 'black marked'. Individuals who have 'responsible' jobs will be subjected to enhanced scrutiny.'

What was happening in China was called a social credit score and I wrote then that it was likely that Western Governments would soon follow suit.

And they are now doing so with great enthusiasm.

It might not have obviously reached your life just yet – but it will, oh it will.

China has led the way because the Chinese system is more ruthlessly efficient than anything the West can offer. The Chinese government has more control over everything and the people don't have much control over anything.

It works very easily.

Everyone starts off with so many points.

And a smart App on every phone measures your behaviour and

helps the authorities decide whether or not you are good citizen.

There are, of course, video cameras absolutely everywhere watching to see whether you cross the road at the wrong time, smoke in public, throw down litter or do anything considered anti-social or inappropriate. If you talk to the wrong sort of people you'll find your credit rating goes down. Stand and talk to me and you'll get black marks. In China cameras have helped the authorities imprison people for 'traveling to sensitive countries'.

China has one camera for every two people and they're equipped with facial recognition technology that can pick an individual out of a football crowd in less time than it takes to say 'surely they can't do that!'

Supermarket cameras and computers watch to see how much you spend on alcohol, cigarettes, sweets and fatty foods. You'll lose points if you spend too much on the wrong sort of food.

Local authorities measure how much recycling you put out, and cameras in the bins will tell computers how much food you've thrown away and how much excess packaging you've had to discard.

Of course, social credit scores are already here in the West and they have been introduced slowly so that we get used to them.

Controls already exist. In the UK for example, drivers of more expensive motor cars have to pay a special, massively increased tax to use a motor car on the roads. That's a blatant punishment for spending a lot on a motor car. Owners of older cars are denied access to city centres. Those drivers are being punished for having elderly vehicles so that's a punishment for being poor.

On the other hand, citizens who drive electric cars do not have to pay anything towards the building, maintenance and repair of roads. They are exempt from the tax because they are considered to be 'good' citizens. Their cars use the roads just as much as cars which are powered with petrol or diesel but they are exempt from paying a road tax. Drivers of petrol or diesel powered cars are punished for being 'bad' citizens and must pay ever-rising annual taxes to pay for the roads. The system ignores the fact that electric cars have been proven to be no better for the environment than petrol or diesel powered cars. Oh, and drive your brand new diesel powered car into a city and you'll have to pay a special penalty (if you're allowed to drive into the centre at all).

I am constantly astonished, bewildered and, I confess, depressed by the deliberate innocence and wilful ignorance of those who refuse to see where we are heading, and who believe (or should that be 'hope') that in a short while everything will go back to the 'old normal'.

Why is it?

My sad conclusion is that the relatively few but naïve commentators, editors and so on who have not been bought by the conspirators simply don't have the questioning nature needed to look critically at the way our world is changing at such a pace. I confess I find it difficult to understand how anyone could have been deceived by the plague fraud (a look at the raw statistics should have demolished any trust in their government's lies) or by the global warming fraud (equally without merit) or the manufactured war in Ukraine (which was obviously detonated by the US and the UK) but I have found it even more alarming to see just the lack of interest in the way our world is being changed by digital ID and social credit.

I'm not being gloomy, I'm not trying to scare you and I'm not being dramatic. I'm telling you the truth. If you think I'm exaggerating, please remember, I've been absolutely accurate about everything that's happened. In 2004 I wrote a book called 'Why Everything Is Going to Get Worse'. I was warning about compulsory vaccination programmes and the medical profession's attacks on the elderly over a decade ago. In 2020, I warned about the danger of digital currencies and the outlawing of cash, the abuse of DNR notices in hospitals, the use of the useless PCR tests to collect DNA samples (that was denied until companies admitted selling the DNA they were harvesting) and the use of the lockdowns to kill millions worldwide and destroy economies.

A year ago I warned that food and fuel prices would go up. Today they are going up almost daily and there's much profiteering I'm afraid.

People laughed when I warned that inflation and interest rates would rocket. Look what's happening now. The UK now owes so much that the interest on the nation's debt costs £83 billion a year. Your taxes are spent paying the interest – let alone the capital.

The conspirators have been following a play book. They've used brain washing and propaganda to take over the world and it hasn't been difficult to work out what comes next. The war is a ruthless, brutal, propaganda war fought with the aid of communist techniques and psy-op tricks devised by the CIA and the US Army. (I've studied the US Army and CIA manuals to see what they're doing and what they're planning.)

Two years ago I provided the evidence that even the Government's advisors knew that the rebranded flu was no worse than the ordinary, common or garden flu. Back in 2020, I provided evidence about the side effects – including myocarditis and clots – of the covid jabs. The sneerers had fun with that but my warnings were absolutely accurate.

Every time I've revealed more truths, the censorship has been tightened up. Telling the truth is now a serious offence.

I've been censored for many years but the censorship has dramatically increased since the fraud began early in 2020.

Wikipedia and Google demonised me with lies and I've been completely banned by all the mainstream media and publishers. I've been banned by YouTube (which even banned me from accessing their site) by Facebook (which two years ago said I was a danger to their community and wouldn't let me join) by Twitter, by LinkedIn and by every other social media outlet that I am aware of. They all claim they favour free speech but they do the opposite. They censor, they crush and they de-platform. They are the enemy. Incidentally, did you know that Google and YouTube have been placed on a red list for child safety because they are endangering children through their censorship?

All of these corrupt sites have banned me permanently for the simple crime of telling the truth and being absolutely accurate. For them to claim they represent free speech is like Wikipedia claiming it's an encyclopaedia when I believe it's more of a protection racket (give an editor money and he'll change an entry according to your wishes) or a platform for government-controlled lies and misdirection. The Royal Society of Arts expelled me as a Fellow. I believe that a BBC employee had complained because I'd been telling the truth. I can see that the BBC might find that rather shocking.

Sharing important truths about covid and global warming can get you into big trouble with the believers and the misinformed and insane global warming alarmists. Governments claim to have been following the science but that, of course, is a lie of brobdingnagian proportions and I can only assume that the science has been under the control of Baron Munchausen.

The 77th brigade, the CIA and government-sponsored hacks go round the internet putting lies and abuse and even death threats wherever they see my name. (And not just me, of course. Other doctors and scientists who have spoken out have also been targeted.) There are fake sites in my name on social media, and although the companies running the platforms know the sites are fake they won't take them down. I have no social media presence. Anything in my name is fake and probably controlled by the 77th brigade or the CIA. The enemy has deliberately and systematically done everything they could do to destroy my life – simply because I have told the truth.

I've still got my websites – where I put up material every day – and there are platforms such as Brand New Tube and BitChute which carry my videos. Mohammad Butt and Brand New Tube were put under tremendous pressure to ban me and had to move their platform out of the UK so that I could continue to make videos for the platform. I'm forever grateful for that. My websites are attacked by hackers thousands of times a month – every month.

Why would the authorities want to silence me if I weren't telling truths they want suppressed? Why won't they debate these issues? Why does the BBC openly refuse to allow any debate about vaccination for example?

Telling the truth is now a punishable offence and what too many people fail to realise is that social credit (the end result of what is happening) is now well on its way and it will soon be unstoppable. We are entering a world of digital dictatorship, total surveillance and trans-humanism.

The first part of this book explains precisely what social credit is and how it works. The second part of the book explains the many singular ways in which our lives will be permanently changed by social credit.

As you read, please remember the words of Margaret Mead: 'Never underestimate the power of a small group of thoughtful, committed citizens to change the world. Indeed it's the only thing that ever has.'

At the moment the conspirators are succeeding in their plan to change the world in the way they want it to be changed.

But we can change it back to the way it was if that's what we want to do.

Vernon Coleman June 2022
Bilbury, England

Part One
What is Social Credit? What does it mean? How does it work?

Politicians, journalists, social scientists, masochists and communists talk about social credit as if it were a 'good thing'.

'I don't know what all the fuss is about,' said one. 'It won't be so bad. In fact, if you behave yourself it will be a good thing.'

A programme promoting social credit on NBC News in the US, stated that social credit pushes people to become better citizens. 'You're not going to be punished if you haven't done anything wrong,' they said, ignoring the fact that it is the Government which decides the definition of wrong.

Well, if you are a fan of totalitarianism or communism then I suppose social credit is a good thing.

However, there is no escaping the fact that social credit is a scheme designed to enable governments to control their citizens. Every new law and rule ties into the social credit system which is now clearly the way in which the Great Reset will be turned into practical reality. It is government policy everywhere to exhaust their citizens with a constant barrage of new rules and regulations (which are backed by force and therefore have the power of law).

And although all this may sound like futuristic science fiction, it isn't. Social credit is here and it is growing by the minute.

Take a look at precisely how social credit operates in China.

The social credit system set up in China was officially introduced in 2014 though it was planned many years before that and given official approval back at the beginning of the 21st century when Shanghai introduced a credit system designed to assess eligibility for loans – in much the same way as has been done in the West for many years. In fact, of course, social ratings and rankings have been used in China for millennia. But what has been happening since 2014 has been happening very quickly. By 2017, there were 8.8 million Chinese citizens listed as debtors on a 'shame' list.

The idea of the system is that information about every individual will be collected together from all possible sources – schools, workplaces, banks, doctors' surgeries, hospitals, police, libraries, supermarkets, internet platforms, travel companies, closed circuit television cameras (usually facial recognition software) and so on. Policemen in China wear facial recognition sunglasses. (Facial recognition technology is used in the USA and according to the Department of Homeland Security, all travellers, whether US citizens or not will be subject to facial recognition technology. A British court ruled in 2019 that biometric face scanners do not violate privacy and human rights, and it is acceptable for the police to use them in the UK.) Chinese stores are planning to use facial recognition cameras so that customers can make purchases simply by looking at a camera. Around 200 million surveillance cameras in China are used in conjunction with artificial intelligence facial recognition cameras. Anyone anywhere in the world who uses a camera which uses facial recognition software should know that their faces will be recorded and stored. It is impossible to have a UK passport without being photographed by a camera which uses software to put your image into storage.

Recognition software can identify people by the way they walk. Smart meters installed in private homes will tell the authorities what time you get up, what time you eat, what you eat, when you go to the loo and when you go to bed. If you get a speeding fine or a parking ticket the details of that offence will be recorded too. Citizens can gain points by being willing to give blood or by proving themselves to be hard workers.

In the Chinese city of Rongcheng, there is a comprehensive grading system which obtains information from 142 different government departments – with hundreds of positive and negative factors being used to create a final score.

The information collected is used to compensate and reward those considered to be model citizens and to punish those regarded as transgressors. The social credit system is designed to enable the authorities to name and shame according to behaviour.

There are several systems in different Chinese provinces, and social credit ratings are measured with a simple points system with, for example, all citizens starting off with 1,000 points and then losing points whenever they 'misbehave'. A citizen's rating will determine whether he or she is rewarded or punished.

The goal of the system is to provide the Government with a general assessment of each individual citizen's trustworthiness. The system also provides an assessment of the trustworthiness of all companies. Companies which helped in the fight against the rebranded flu (by donating medical supplies) were rewarded and placed on a 'green list' which ensured that administrative problems were streamlined. On the other hand companies which charged too much for essential items or which breached quarantine rules were penalised. Businesses which have poor scores are likely to be subjected to extra audits or government inspectors. Businesses which have good scores are likely to have goods moved through customs more quickly.

'Good' citizens, who have obeyed instructions and behaved impeccably will be rewarded in many ways – such as by being allowed to travel, use a public library, rent bicycles or borrow money and by being entitled to send their children to better schools, to obtain a better quality of health care or to apply for (and be given) better jobs. Buying green vegetables, sensible clothing and nappies will all boost a citizen's rating. Buy sensible work shoes with good soles and a long life potential and your rating will rise. Those who praise the Government will see their rating improve. Those who report citizens who have criticised the Government, or any part of it, will be rewarded for their loyalty to the State. If you donate blood, perform charitable works, praise the Government regularly on social media and help those poorer than yourself then you will rewarded.

'Bad' citizens, who have shown themselves to be rebellious, deceitful or disobedient in any way, will be punished by being named and shamed on the internet and elsewhere and by being denied access to travel, hotels, restaurants, good schools, good hospitals and good jobs. 'Bad' citizens may also be banned from entering shopping malls or food stores and may, therefore, be denied access to food.

What else makes you a 'bad' citizen?

Well, buying meat, chocolates, alcohol or frivolous clothing will damage your rating as will playing games on the internet. Buy a pair of high heel shoes or inappropriately expensive trainers and you will lose points. If your home is not considered energy compliant you will be punished. You will lose points if you burn your own logs on an open fire or in a log burner because that will pollute the atmosphere (and give you independence).

(In the UK log burners are 'bad' and you must use expensive electricity produced by burning pellets of wood which have been obtained by chopping down trees several thousand miles away, turning the logs into pellets and then transporting the pellets thousands of miles by diesel powered ship and lorry.)

If Chinese citizens write or say something rude about their government they will lose points. Those who fail to visit their parents regularly are punished as are jaywalkers, those who smoke in non-smoking zones and those who walk a dog without putting it on a lead. Government employees will remove a dog if its leftover food isn't cleared away. And the former dog owner will be banned from having another animal for five years. Senior citizens can sue their children if they don't visit regularly. Not sorting your personal waste properly is a sin as is swearing in public. Spying on your friends, relatives and neighbours will be rewarded; so, for example, reporting friends, relatives and neighbours for using bad language will win you brownie points. If someone is in debt (and everyone will know if they are because the information will be online) anyone who thinks they could pay off their debt can gain themselves points by reporting them. All internet data (including searches) is used to compile social credit ratings, and players who cheat in online video games are punished by having their social credit rating reduced. If you spread rumours on the internet you will classified as a bad person. If your apologies for your transgressions are considered insincere you will be punished. If you have your PCR tests done regularly then you will be rewarded but if you miss your testing appointments you will lose points. If you have the vaccinations you are told to have then you will be rewarded. But if you choose not to have a particular vaccination then you will lose points. Those who do not pay bills on time will be punished though taxes and utility bills will be paid automatically, with the appropriate sums simply deducted from the citizen's account. If there is insufficient money in the account the citizen will lose yet more points. Those in debt for whatever reason will end up in a downward spiral.

(Before I go any further, I should mention by the way that some years ago I wrote a column in a large circulation Chinese newspaper. One week I wrote a column criticising vaccination. Within hours of the column appearing I received a note from the editor sacking me from the paper. And within a couple of days after that I received an email from my Chinese publisher telling me that they were no longer allowed to sell my books (several of which had been long-term bestsellers in China). I was also told that neither they nor any other publisher in China would be allowed to publish any of my books. Later they wrote to tell me that the Chinese Government had ruled that in future no Chinese publisher would be allowed to publish health books written by Western authors.)

In 2019, it was suggested that 23 million people in China had been blacklisted from travelling by train or aeroplane because they had low social credit ratings. Many students were prevented from attending schools or universities because their parents had poor scores or because one parent was on a debtor's list. Employers are able to consult blacklists before hiring new employees or handing out contracts – and are encouraged to do so.

Highly rated taxpayers get their tax returns processed more speedily. Lowly rated individuals have to pay higher insurance premiums.

Once someone is on a blacklist in one area of the country they are likely to be blacklisted in other provinces. And once someone is on a blacklist it usually takes between two to five years to be removed. Citizens on blacklists must prove that they have changed their erring ways. The system is also used to spot potentially harmful behaviour before it occurs.

In China, everyone now lives in a point scoring computer game. Citizens who don't adapt their lifestyle to suit the requirements of the Government will be severely punished. If a member of a Chinese citizen's family or partner has low scores then they must avoid them – or their points score will be reduced. Think about that: the system ensures that the friends and relatives of individuals who behave in a way that the State considers unacceptable will lose points from their credit rating.

In short, those who do as they are told will be rewarded and those who disobey will be punished. Individual citizens will be able to check on their status by looking at their points total. And, remember, individuals who are regarded as 'bad' citizens will be named and shamed on posters, on television and, of course, on the internet.

The aim of all this is that citizens will be encouraged to behave in an 'acceptable' fashion and will, therefore, be constantly aware of their behaviour – constantly aware that if they cross a street when not allowed, or park a vehicle where they are not allowed to park, they will lose points on their credit rating. (The vehicle will probably be rented because ownership of vehicles will be very limited.)

The Chinese social credit system (upon which the social credit systems being introduced in the rest of the world are based) is built upon a network of computers and requires citizens to carry with them, and to use, smart phones which are equipped with apps connecting them to a central bureaucracy. Smart TVs, computers, iPads, cell phones and so on collect data by recording conversations, movements and user activity. Video games use facial recognition software. It is no surprise that phone companies are planning to phase out phones which use 2G and 3G technology which do not transmit as much private information to corporate and governmental data banks. Owners of 2G and 3G phones will simply wake up one day and find that their phones no longer work.

Advanced cameras can reveal a good deal about the behaviour of an individual and uncover secrets and thought crimes. Back in 2011, it was possible to decode brain activity associated with watching movies and the technology is improving day by day. Digital assistants on smart phones and televisions record all sounds and conversations. Players who use the Pokémon GO game might not realise that they are paying to be watched and followed. Blockchain was promoted as an anti-establishment tool but it's the opposite. Cryptocurrencies are popular with governments (many of which are introducing their own) because they help get rid of cash and control behaviour.

It is this system which is now being rolled out throughout the world.

The astonishing thing is that the vast majority of the well-educated classes cannot see what is happening. They aren't all conspirators, in on the scam, but many have closed their eyes and ears to the truth. Why? Money. They have been bought. Doctors have been bought with huge, excessively large fees for giving jabs they must have known did not work and were not safe. Many doctors around the world were well paid to appear in advertisements and to promote treatments they should have known were both ineffective and unsafe. Journalists have been bought with the huge amounts of money paid by governments to the publishers and TV stations for which they work. Drug company staff made huge fortunes out of the jabs they sold. Around the world, ministers and their relatives made huge sums out of supplying masks, gloves and other equipment to hospitals. Civil servants and many others were allowed to work from home and do little or no work. Millions were given huge furlough payments to stay at home and do no work. Others were given up to £50,000 to invest in their businesses, with many apparently assuming that the money was a gift to do with as they liked. In the UK, the cost of the official largesse alone is well in excess of £400 billion.

It is not surprising that so many said nothing as the greatest fraud in the history of the world was allowed to unfold and as the 'principles' and structure of the Great Reset were promoted. Indeed, as the story has rapidly unfolded many commentators have chosen to look for other explanations for events that were, in reality, part of the Great Reset. They have, for example, blamed the collapse in the global economy and the rise in inflation on the financial crisis of 2007/8 – ignoring the fake pandemic, the absurd demands of the net zero aficionados and the global warming cultists and the sanctions against Russia brought in during the spring of 2022.

So, what has all this got to do with me, you might well ask. Surely the Chinese system won't really affect the rest of the world.

Well, in September 2020, when most of the population were still wondering if they dared nip out to the one open local shop to buy a can of beans, and wondering if it would be legal to buy a loaf of bread as well, the UK Government published something called 'Evidence and Scenarios for Global Data Systems – the Future of Citizens Data Systems'.

The Chinese Government had by then been using its social credit system to prioritise its national economy and to take control of its citizens and the British Government, not wanting to be left out, but not wanting to terrify a population that had already been systematically and deliberately scared half to death, promised that it would 'harness data to boost growth and productivity, to improve public services and to inform a new wave of scientific research'.

That's the sort of promise that sounds wonderful until you read it again and think what it means.

Similar systems to the one I've described in China are already in action in other countries, and though the schemes are young and, in human terms, just learning to walk, they do have a quiet menace about them that I find deeply disquieting.

For example, New Zealanders who go to Australia are entitled to live and work there for life unless they fail a 'good character' test in which case they will be deported. The good character test is decided entirely at the discretion of officials. (In one case a 15-year-old child was deported). There is also a 'ParentsNext' welfare programme which provides payments to single mothers but to qualify for the money a single mother must show that she has undertaken certain activities with her children – such as visiting the public library or attending swimming lessons. Doesn't that sound familiar?

In Bologna, Italy, the authorities have introduced a 'smart citizens' wallet'. Holders receive digital points to spend or use to obtain discounts for virtuous behaviour (such as enthusiastic recycling).

As governments in the West declared their enthusiastic support for Ukraine in its war with Russia, Ukraine quietly announced that it is the first country to implement the World Economic Forum's Great Reset by setting up a social credit App combining universal basic income, digital ID and a vaccine passport in a single App. You thought the Ukrainians were busy dodging bombs but they had time to set up the Schwab pleasing App. Why else do you think the conspirators are rewarding them by sending arms and money? Why do you think you are being asked to send them any money, tanks, ammunition and old jumpers you have lying around at the back of the garage?

In France, within two days of his re-election, President Macron introduced a Digital Identity Guarantee so that citizens of France could have a digital ID card complying with the EU's European Digital Identity package. The vaccine passport gave birth to the digital ID and this, tied in with the digital currencies produced by Central Banks, gives the conspirators total control.

In Canada, the Government has a new advisory group to enforce censorship and to regulate what they decide is harmful content. The Government has given itself the sole authority to decide what is disinformation and what can be regarded as a conspiracy theory. In Quebec, a special tax was introduced for those who had been wise enough not to have the covid-19 jab.

In Vienna, Austria, where the un-jabbed were subjected to special lockdowns and there was a push towards 'no jab, no job' every citizen will be offered an App which will reward good behaviour with 'Vienna Tokens'. There has been no official notice of what constitutes 'good' behaviour and what constitutes 'bad' behaviour but the App will certainly recognise each individual's travel behaviour – whether they travel by foot, bicycle or public transport. The scheme is funded by the European Research Council (which has links to the World Economic Forum). The plan is to turn Vienna into a smart city with data replacing money as the city's currency. The aim is that in future all decisions will be made by artificial intelligence so that there will be no need for elections. In other words, behavioural data will replace democracy. Private property will not be encouraged and will, indeed be a luxury.

In Germany, citizens have a SCHUFA score which is necessary for buying or renting a house or receiving goods on credit. The SCHUFA system tracks each citizen's entire credit history. It has been claimed that someone who lives in a poor area, or has low scoring neighbours, will find that their score is lowered. Scores may also be lowered if relatives have poor scores. Also, in Germany, some health insurance providers use fitness data to reduce insurance premiums.

In Russia in 2018, the Moscow Times reported that by 2025, four out of five Russians will have been given a 'personal development trajectory – a digital file which will contain every achievement in a person's life – 'the misses, mistakes, big projects'. The aim is to digitize the Russian economy and roll out digital technologies nationwide.

In Zimbabwe 'people who peddle information deemed false by the Government face up to 20 years in prison, a hefty fine or both.'

In Thailand, the Government warned that 'anybody joking about the virus could face up to five years prison time'.

In the Philippines, the unjabbed who left their homes were threatened with prison.

In Holland, a Dutch bank (Rabobank) links customer spending habits with their CO_2 emissions, though, as far as I know, quite what this has to do with the bank hasn't been explained.

Denmark developed a covid-19 digital passport so that Danish nationals can travel freely around the world. The corollary is that those without the passport can't travel freely around the world.

In Ireland, the Government has stated that The State 'shall delimit the right to private property where it is necessary to ensure the common good'.

Iran has introduced digital food rationing based on biometric IDs.

The word 'sequestration' now appears often in many countries.

In Wales, selected citizens will be given the national average wage. They will be allowed to keep the money (believed to be around £20,000 a year) on top of anything they earn. But if they don't want to do any work they don't have to. This is an absurdly generous version of Universal Basic Income. (I can't help wondering how much services to other citizens will have to be cut in order to pay for this social experiment.)

India has a program known as 'Aadhaar' which means that each resident has a 12 digit number. Each individual has their fingerprints and iris scans stored. The system was introduced to check entitlement to welfare programs but is used for law enforcement purposes and there are suggestions that information has been sold for commercial purposes.

The US Government gave billions of dollars of taxpayers' money to the mainstream media to promote the covid jabs and to maintain the Government-sponsored myths and to spread misinformation. Experts and celebrities and media doctors were hired and fear based survivor stories were published. Vaccine enthusiast Bill Gates contributed $319 million to the media, with grants to journalists. (Gates, of course, has financial links with the BBC and The Guardian newspaper in the UK.) The Central Intelligence Agency infiltrated the media, bribed journalists to publish fake stories and is believed to have been responsible for converting Wikipedia (and therefore Google) into demonising tools to attack truth-telling doctors and scientists. The US Department of Homeland Security has openly stated that conspiracy theorists and anyone questioning what the Government says about covid is an 'extremist'.

And International Monetary Fund researchers have called for internet search history to be tied to credit scores.

In the UK, the Government (which has also given millions of pounds of taxpayers' money to the media) has a 'nudge unit' (officially known as the Behavioural Insights Team of psychologists) which exists to create fear and shame and promote group think. The

Government advisors regularly pushed for more terror and more fear. A known communist called Susan Michie, wanted more rules and more fear. The UK Government also talked of introducing surveillance drones, ostensibly to protect women who left their homes for whatever reason. Oppressive new laws are being introduced and inconvenient truths are dangerous, say the politicians and the media, and those spreading them must be suppressed. Councils now warn homeowners that 'failing to register (to vote) can have a negative impact on your credit score'. The UK Digital Identity and Attitudes Trust Framework, part of the nationwide digital ID push, enabled citizens to prove their ID using digital methods instead of having to rely on traditional physical documents. Citizens were able to 'create a digital identity with a trusted organisation' (I cannot think of any organisations anywhere which I would describe as 'trusted'). The 'trusted organisation' would be given a 'legal gateway' to 'carry out verification checks against official data held by public bodies'. This new scheme was promoted as being useful to check job applicants and those wanting to rent property.

In August 2021, the UK Government announced that a new App would monitor shopping habits and encourage healthy eating. Supermarket purchases will be assessed by new software, and citizens will be rewarded if they buy healthy foods and punished if they buy foods considered bad for them. Buy a six pack and a bumper bag of crisps and Big Brother will decide that you are a bad person. Big Brother will be watching everything you do.

Also in the UK, a major bank called Santander, made it virtually impossible to bank online without using a mobile phone. Those who complained, either because they had no mobile phone or had a poor signal, were told to visit a branch. But, of course, most branches had been shut.

Cinemas in the UK are planning to introduce digital ID cards for children to prevent them seeing films that contain sex and violence. The digital ID App will confirm the age of a child as uploaded from a passport. The Government has approved the use of the digital ID to enable children to access money from child trust funds. Three million Britons have already downloaded the digital ID App – with children and young adults the most enthusiastic users.

And there is a good deal of oppressive new legislation being introduced in the UK. The 'Police, Crime, Sentencing and Courts Bill' will end the right of the people to protest peacefully and lead the nation further into a police state. If a dozen bird watchers gather together to look at a Lesser Spotted Tweetle bird, they'll probably be arrested. If boy scouts go camping the police can (and probably will) round them up and arrest them.

The Human Rights Act Reform Bill, is officially called a Modern Bill of Rights includes mention of the Magna Carta but, paradoxically, this is a bill which King John would have loved. They're pushing it as a bill for freedom but that's like claiming the BBC provides balanced, fair-minded news programmes. The UK Government says freedom of speech and academic freedom are fundamental principles but, like governments everywhere, it has suppressed both. The UK Government adds that freedom of expression cannot be an absolute right when balanced against the need to protect national security. That's their excuse for lying, for demonising the truth-tellers and for suppressing facts and truths.

And don't forget the UK's Emergency Bill, introduced in March 2020, immediately after the UK Government was officially told that the rebranded flu was no more deadly than the flu. It still stands in the background and gives the Government extraordinary powers. It enables them to do pretty much whatever they like. Parliament keeps voting it through.

And then there is NHSX – a special little organisation which is linking the NHS and NHS Digital. The plan is to introduce technical architecture (as they call it) to link the whole of the NHS – across health and caring. There will be apps taking the vax passports directly into digital passports. Privacy will be a thing of the past. Once again this is being done very quietly by unelected bureaucrats. In the new NHS, the medical establishment wants a reduction in the number of cancer screening tests being done and the number of people being treated. Cutting down patients being diagnosed and treated will, they say, help stop global warming. The latest idiotic idea from the Government is to declare yet another war on cancer with a cancer vaccine as the weapon.

When warned about the coming lack of privacy, millions glibly say 'I've got nothing to hide'. But I wonder if they'll still say that when their neighbours can peep at the pictures of their piles which they sent to their doctor. And how thrilled will they be that their neighbours can see exactly how much they've got in the bank. That's what digital passports mean.

Also in the UK, Government departments, including HMRC, have introduced fiendishly complicated systems of verification which are impossible for many to use. It's all part of the plan to tie citizens into a sophisticated digital identification programme.

Everywhere in the world, the conspirators are fighting to gain power over us all. Obtaining and keeping complete power is an essential part of the Great Reset and the move towards a world dominated by the principles of social credit.

Life for the 'good citizens' will be just like life in the USSR and China. It will be like life in a communist State. It will be like life in a giant prison camp. 'Good' citizens who do as they are told to do will be entitled to buy cheap food, rent cheap apartments, take cheap holidays and get jobs with light work. They will be entitled to free education for their children and free medical care too. The 'good' citizens will be given security and shelter in return for their freedom, their independence and their free will.

In the now infamous words associated with Klaus Schwab and the World Economic Forum, the 'good' citizens will own nothing and they will be happy.

For now they say that all this is voluntary, of course.

They promise that you will not be punished if you do nothing wrong.

The first problem is that doing nothing wrong is difficult to define.

The second problem is some people would not regard these schemes as entirely voluntary, and nor would they agree that people are not punished for not complying. In the UK, for example, home owners who do not agree to have a smart meter fitted to measure and control their electricity supply may be denied access to the cheapest forms of electricity and may find that their bills are much higher than those of compliant citizens who agree to have a smart meter in their homes and who are therefore allowed access to cheaper tariffs. It is because of digitalisation that bank branches and GP services are being closed. What is the need for banks or surgery premises when everything can be done online, through a constantly monitored computer of some kind. Closing bank branches forces customers to go online.

The basic problem with social credit is that we are no longer dealing with an ordinary assessment of what is right and what is wrong. (With kindness being right and murder or theft being wrong.) We are talking about 'good' and 'bad' being decided arbitrarily by bureaucrats who, for example, will argue that people who sort their rubbish satisfactorily are 'good' whereas people whose recycling skills are not considered adequate are 'bad'.

The world of social credit gets absolutely everywhere; it's more intrusive and tougher to remove than hogweed.

If you live in a house that is bigger than you need then you will be marked down and your taxes will rise. If you have spare rooms you'll be punished. If you do a useful job and give money to charity you'll get extra points. If you criticise the Government then you'll lose points.

When you're away from home, the authorities will, of course, know where you are all the time.

Indeed, if you behave badly you won't be allowed to go far from home. If you haven't obeyed all the health regulations you won't be allowed to travel on public transport, fly anywhere or go abroad.

If your social credit rating goes down you won't be able to borrow money, buy a house or book a decent room in a hotel.

If your rating goes down too far you won't be allowed to go into hospital and if you get in by accident, they'll slam a Do Not Resuscitate notice around your neck before you can say 'what's that for?'

You'll receive bonus points if you live in a tiny, modern, poorly built flat with thin walls and absolutely no privacy but you'll lose those points if you keep a pet or complain about absolutely anything.

If you spend too much on clothes or shoes your rating will go down, and saving money will mark you out as guilty of something or other and you won't be able to hire a car, get a promotion at work, use a gym or get your children into a school with textbooks.

If you are a lot of trouble, and rude about the authorities, you'll find that your internet speeds will slow to a crawl, and if you have your own business and talk back to council officials, you won't get any help with planning problems or be able to obtain any official government contracts.

If you don't dress appropriately when out in public, or are spotted crossing the road when the lights are against you, then you'll be photographed and your picture displayed on the internet. If you have a row with a neighbour then your pictures will be put on a billboard near your home and you'll be shamed. If you are late with your taxes you'll be marked down for regular audits, your business will be inspected once a week and your picture will appear on a shame board on the internet. And you'll find it impossible to obtain licences, permits and loans you might need.

In recent years it has become necessary for almost everyone to have a licence before being allowed to get a job. Taxi drivers and dental hygienists need licences. In some countries, even hairdressers, dog groomers, and beauticians need to buy a licence. The only people who aren't required to have licences (or training of any kind) are politicians. And they are the only people who really need them. Demanding that workers buy a licence makes them vulnerable. The State which hands out the licence can easily take it away if the licence holder has a low social credit rating.

In restaurants the cameras will study your manners and your eating habits and the amount of food you leave on the plate – all likely to damage your social credit rating.

Snitches, sneaks, police officers and over-compliant government employees will mark you down for any sin of commission or omission.

By now you probably think I'm making this up and I wish I were but I'm not. We're not talking about the far distant future. We're talking about things that are happening now, or about to happen in the very new future.

You'll receive points if you give blood, lose points if you associate with people with low scores, be punished if you spend frivolously or don't praise the Government on social media.

Eating meat or indulging in unsuitable activities will result in a severe points loss, as will putting too much refuse into public bins. Facial recognition cameras in bins will see and punish you and reduce your food credit.

Not having the correct number of children, being overweight and owning land will result in a loss of social credit points (unless you own a very great deal of land). In the UK the Office for National Statistics has already claimed that childless women will be a burden on the State because they'll have no one to look after them. So they'll be punished too.

Chronic sickness, mental illness, being old and being disabled will lose you points as will being arrested (it doesn't matter whether you are not found guilty).

Having too big a carbon footprint, being middle class or white or asking too many questions will all result in a loss of points as will being too protective of your family.

You'll lose social credit points if you cause some 'identity harm', say something that makes someone feel uncomfortable about who they are, where they are from or what they look like – or don't say something that causes them to feel good.

If you show any micro-aggression, exhibit white privilege or stir up hatred, you'll be punished. If you behave in a threatening or abusing or insulting manner, you will be in trouble, as you will if you communicate threatening abusive or insulting material to another person or if another person fears that you might threaten them or not like them. In the UK, it is already a crime to take a dog for a walk without a lead if someone who sees you says that they were uncomfortable with the presence of your dog or alarmed by its presence. (For details, see the UK Government website).

Your intention will be irrelevant. The complainant only has to say he was hurt or alarmed or frightened.

Writers, actors or film or stage directors will be vulnerable if anyone finds any of their material offensive. I suspect that plays by Shakespeare won't appear much in the future.

You probably think I'm really kidding now. If you do, just check out what is happening in Scotland where the police now define a crime or incident as 'hateful' based on the perception of the victim (and not on the intent of the offender). And naturally, the police and politicians have been encouraging citizens to snitch on those breaking laws.

You can get into serious trouble for playing loud music or having trees in your garden. They say trees are bad because they may interfere with communications and have no practical purpose (though a year or two ago we were told they were essential to save the polar bears). There will be no place for aesthetics or nature in the new world order. You can get into serious trouble for feeding the birds in your own garden if someone objects.

What else will be bad?

Eating on public transport, missing a medical appointment,

parking in the wrong place, missing a job interview and jaywalking will all lose you points and make your life more difficult.

If you think I've gone mad you should know that cybersecurity experts have discovered that 32% of adults between 25 and 34 in 21 countries (a total of 10,000 individuals) have already had difficulty getting a mortgage or loan because of their social media activity.

A fairly scary survey found that two thirds of individuals are willing to share information about themselves or others to get a shopping discount while half are willing to do so if it helps them skip queues at airports. One in two individuals says they are happy for the Government to monitor everyone's social media behaviour if it means keeping the public safe.

Of course, it will be impossible to find out what your social credit score is, to find out exactly how scores are made up or to correct any error. And scores will be changed in real time. So you could join a queue thinking you are entitled to hire a car or board a train and find, when you get to the front of the queue, that your rating has changed and you can't do either of those things.

Governments, big companies and local authorities are already gathering information about you from facial recognition cameras, biometric studies at airports, drones, surveillance planes and social media. This is the technocratic state in full fly. Using a silly name or avatar on social media will provide you with absolutely no protection. They know exactly who stinkyfeet of Weymouth really is and they know the name, address and inside leg measurement of bumfluff from Colorado.

You can forget about privacy, freedom or rights.

We will soon all be living in China.

If one person in a family breaks the law, the whole family will be punished.

Taking an active part in a religious ceremony will result in punishment. You may, for example, be sent to an education and training centre where the inmates study political propaganda.

Every time you give information online they are storing up information about you, your views, your personality and so on. So far around 4.5 billion people around the world use the internet and most have social media accounts.

And there are, in truth, so, so many ways in which your social credit score can be adversely affected.

All this is known as social engineering. It's something politicians have been trying to do for many years since, when it works, which it does, it gives them complete control over the population. There is no longer any need to worry about opposition or criticism.

In China, citizens who do 'good' things for the State and their community are rewarded by having their photographs and names on a local wall. This is exactly what I remember seeing in East Germany in the 1970s. And back then people vied with one another to please the State and win a place on the wall.

If you want to know the sort of society you and your children are going to live in then look at China now – where what people do, say and think is being constantly monitored.

We are moving rapidly into a dystopian, digital dictatorship.

Good behaviour will be rewarded and bad behaviour punished. But who defines what is good and what is bad?

Geotracking is the new normal now. Your financial records are combined with your criminal record, academic record, medical record and shopping patterns. They're keeping an eye on the type of friends you have, the videos you watch, the people you date or marry or meet.

This is Big Brother on speed

In the Brave New World, those with a low credit score won't be able to move an inch.

People who speak out about corruption or who question the propaganda will be punished. If they are fined then their fine will be higher because they are seen as bad people.

And it's already all happening.

Computer games are training us for our future.

Remember, I'm completely banned in China because I wrote a column for a Chinese newspaper which contained factually accurate information on vaccination. The column was considered unacceptable. My books in Chinese were instantly removed from sale.

I leave you with the following fact.

There are public loos in China which won't let you in without first checking your face and identifying you. Only then will the machine dispense the small quantity of loo paper you are allowed.

How many sheets will you be allowed if you have a low credit score? Two? One? None at all?

You may be smiling now.
But see if you're still smiling in twelve months' time.

Part Two
How will Social Credit change your life?

In this part of the book I'm going to explore some of the ways in which social credit can, and will, affect the way you live your life.

Animals

Things started to go wrong when feeding the birds became a crime. The excuse was that birds spread disease to humans but wild birds are no more likely to spread disease than cage birds and no one suggested that budgies should be banned. People have taken pleasure from feeding the birds for centuries but the conspirators don't like wild creatures and they don't like people having fun. In Paris, a few years ago I bought bird seed at a supermarket. The woman on the checkout wanted to know why I was buying bird food. Foolishly, I told her I intended to feed the pigeons. She was furious and berated me. It was too late because the bird food was in my bag. When I went back to the supermarket the next day, every packet of bird food had been removed from the shelves. The manager told me they weren't selling bird food anymore.

And herein lies a contradiction.

The conspirators want to re-wild huge parts of every country (releasing wild animals into huge areas to ensure that the land isn't used for farming or recreation) but they also want to empty our towns and cities of birds and they want to get rid of farm animals and pets.

Farm animals have to go because the plan is to ensure that we will eat only laboratory designed and factory grown food. Tens of millions of chickens have already been destroyed, allegedly because of the risk of bird flu spreading. Fish and wild deer are also being destroyed to protect us from unnamed diseases. (All this is being done deliberately to increase food shortages).

Pets have to go because there will be no room for dogs, cats or other animals when we are living in small flats in high rise buildings. The clampdown on keeping cats has already started in some countries. Cat owners have been told that they must keep their animals permanently indoors. The conspirators really don't like the idea of people keeping pets. In May 2022, it was suggested that because of the monkey pox scare, it might be necessary to cull guinea pigs, hamsters and other children's pets. Dogs and cats may also have to be culled. (The word 'culled' is, of course, a politically acceptable way of saying 'slaughtered'.)

And bees are disappearing because the conspirators don't want plants to be pollinated.

It isn't just animals that we are losing.

Ironically, trees (once said to be essential to protect us from global warming) are being removed from towns and cities because they get in the way of 5G signals.

All this is being done because of the Great Reset – and the determination to control everything we do, everything we eat, where we live and how we live.

You can tell what the plan is from the fact that in some countries home owners with gardens are already forbidden to grow their own food.

Bank of England

The Bank of England and HM Treasury in the UK are now preparing a UK digital currency to replace cash – and to enable them to know what you are buying, and where and when you are buying it.

The new system is being designed to enable the tax authorities to take money out of your account so that all your taxes and fines are all paid automatically.

All this is being done under the auspices of, and with the encouragement of the Bank of International Settlements, which is very keen on central banks creating digital currencies. It was the Bank of International Settlements which helped fund the Nazis in

World War II. If you want the proof just take a look at my book on the subject – 'The Shocking History of the EU' – in which I pointed out that without the BIS there would have been no Second World War and there would be no European Union. The BIS is mega powerful and it is clearly a big player in the Great Reset and the plans for the new normal.

It's pretty clear that this is part of the social credit program, whereby the authorities will be able to punish or reward you according to your behaviour. If you buy sugary food or meat you will be punished by not being able to travel. If you access the wrong websites, or mix with the wrong people, you will be punished by being denied access to certain shops selling luxuries such as food and clothing.

It's already happening in China and it's coming here. It's an extension of the vax passport scheme. Without a digital passport you won't exist. You'll be like a citizen in the USSR or the Eastern Bloc, trying to exist without papers.

Am I exaggerating?

Not a bit of it. And here's the killer.

The Bank of England and UK Government says that their new digital money will be programmable.

And what do they mean by that?

Well, in their words, (and this how they are planning to sell the new currency to the millions who have accepted social distancing, masks, lockdowns and the experimental jab) parents who give their children pocket money will be able to 'program the money so that it couldn't be used for sweets'.

That's not me talking. That's the Bank of England talking.

Parents will be able to program the new digital currency so that it can't be used to buy sweets.

The digital currency parents will give to children will be the same digital currency that you will receive as part of your universal basic income. It's what your employer will pay you in. It's what your pension or your dividends will be paid in. All automatically put into your bank account and registered in your digital passport.

Those who think that cash is old-fashioned and that digital currencies are wonderful might like to think about all this.

The UK Government is also setting up a Single Customer Account for us all that will 'remove some of their administrative burden by enabling third parties, such as banks and pension providers, to pass on information regarding tax automatically to HMRC.' (HMRC is the tax office in the UK.) Once that is done HMRC will take what it thinks it is owed from your digital account. 'To make life simpler,' they say.

A few years ago Britons rejected Tony Blair's ID cards. This is ID cards on steroids.

And the BIS says that central banks which control their own digital currencies will have absolute control over all rules and regulations.

The Bank of England's new digital currency is part of the social credit system; part of the digital currency world and the digital ID they're forcing on us.

They're going to fix the fake currency so that you can't use it to buy booze if you are an alcoholic and you can't buy chocolate if you're overweight. There will be no fast cars or racing bikes for anyone.

The digital currency will make it very easy for you to pay all your taxes and utility debts because they'll just help themselves to whatever they want.

And the new government-controlled digital money will mean that you can't buy anything if you're considered a bad person.

And just who is a bad person?

I'm afraid that's easy to answer. A bad person is anyone who doesn't have their jab or wear their mask.

Anyone who reads a banned book, visits a proscribed website or watches a video prohibited by the mainstream media is a 'bad' person.

Finally, I feel I should point out that in May 2022, it was announced that Bank of England staff had to go to work one day a week. Earlier, it had been announced that the Bank of England's former employees would receive over an 11% rise in their pension payments. ('Ordinary' old aged pensioners received a 3% rise.)

BBC

The BBC (British Broadcasting Corporation) is a discredited establishment mouthpiece. The organisation is financially associated with Bill Gates, a conspirator, vaccine promoter and friend and associate of Jeffrey Epstein. The BBC is the conspirators' official propaganda unit; it is not a broadcaster – it is a narrowcaster, specialising in propaganda for the conspirators. When you only give one side of the story you are a propagandist not a news organisation.

The BBC specialises in giving air time to people who don't know what the heck they are talking about, while boasting that they never give air time to qualified experts who might have something worthwhile to contribute.

For example, I believe the BBC betrayed the British people by broadcasting a disgraceful video in which parents and children were assured that the covid jab was 100% safe. I'm not aware of any pharmaceutical product which is 100% safe. Was this an error resulting from appalling ignorance? Or was the error deliberate? I can't think of a third explanation.

Why didn't the so-called fact checkers attack the BBC?

I challenged the BBC to produce the name of a single expert they've used who does not have links to the drug industry or to Gates or to the Government and who is not, therefore, open to accusations of prejudice.

The BBC did not reply to the challenge, of course.

In July 2021, I put the following on my websites:

'A BBC employee has apparently complained because a brave and honest man in the street called him a traitor.

I fear the BBC staff who complained when they are called traitors are rather mistaken – I believe that anyone who works for the BBC is a traitor.

Since there are 22,000 people on the BBC payroll – plus an enormous number of part-timers, freelancers and guests – there are at least 22,000 traitors working there. If you work for an organisation which has proved itself to be treacherous then you are, by definition, guilty of treachery; you are a traitor. Those who chose to join the Nazi party could hardly claim innocence when the courts started beckoning. BBC staffers were not conscripted or forced to work for the world's most evil propaganda machine; they chose to work for a corporation which boasts that it refuses to allow debate about vaccination and which suppresses truths.

If the BBC staff members buy themselves a dictionary they'll find that a traitor is someone who betrays people or a principle.

And since the BBC has repeatedly betrayed the public and its own charter – to provide honest, independent news – then they are all traitors. The BBC is a propaganda unit and not a news organisation.

The UK Prime Minister was apparently shocked that a BBC employee should be treated badly by a member of the public.

Johnson said: 'all journalists should be able to carry out their work without intimidation or impediment'.

Well, that's a fine thought, Mr Johnson.

How about applying the same rule to those of us who have been telling the truth since the start of this fraud?

We have been abused, lied about, intimidated, impeded, demonised, monstered, libelled and suppressed.

We have been denied all access to the BBC – which has refused to debate the issues or to share the facts with the public.

So-called journalists who continue to work for the BBC and mainstream media can expect much worse than being called traitors.

They are going to be arrested, tried and imprisoned for helping to promote the biggest fraud in history.

Please remember: don't give money to the BBC. Don't break the law, of course, but don't pay the BBC licence fee. Giving money to the BBC today is as unforgiveable as it would have been to give money to Hitler during World War II.

Today, the BBC is, rightly, more hated than at any time in history. No one should pay the BBC licence fee – avoid it legally, of course, but don't give them a penny. The BBC agreed not to charge the over 75s a licence fee but reneged on the deal. That sort of crookery is the BBC way of doing things.

Remember that the BBC, like that pathetic, down market tabloid rag 'The Guardian', has financial links with the Gates Foundation.

Black Lives Matter

I don't believe that getting rid of statues and history has anything to do with racism, slavery or cultural history. I do believe that it is all part of the conspirators' plan to erase national identities. If the demonstrators really cared about black lives they'd be fighting to stop the starvation and mass deaths in Africa which result from the activities which have taken place since the spring of 2020 – particularly the sanctions against Russia.

How many of the sports people who take a knee before matches are even aware that hundreds of millions of children are starving to death because of what has happened in the last two years?

I wonder how many of those pulling down statues remember that in Orwell's '1984' the obedient party members tore down monuments to civil war soldiers.

Brexit

Brexit (Britain leaving the European Union) was vigorously and dishonestly opposed by a coterie of rabid individuals who were called remainers. The remainers were fighting to keep Britain in the EU for ideological reasons. Ironically, of course, that was the main reason that Brexit was supported. Those wanting to leave the EU were driven by a different ideology but it was an ideology rather than anything else.

The remainers who led the fight to keep the UK within the European Union were supporters of the Great Reset – and I suspect they were led by graduates of WEF placed in positions of power. The conspirators and their defenders and collaborators were desperately upset about Britain leaving the EU because the EU was a first but important step towards the development of a world government.

The remainers (members of the establishment and their acolytes who are devoted to the European Union) used their standard weapons (lies, threats and fears) and accused everyone opposing the European Union of being racist and ignorant and just about everything that they themselves were.

Sadly, Brexit has clearly failed miserably for the simple reason that no one in the Tory Government now supports it. I suspect that Prime Minister Boris Johnson jumped on the Brexit bandwagon because he saw how popular Brexit had become, and with the slick, ruthless, self-serving opportunism which is, apart from a total disconnect from truth, his signature style, realised that he could use it to help him win an election. Since then Johnson has done nothing to make Brexit work and everything to stop it working. The old arguments are being resurrected, supported by the economic chaos caused by the so-called plague fraud, the global warming nonsenses and the sanctions against Russia. Naturally, all the blame for rising prices and general chaos is blamed on Brexit.

It is, therefore, no surprise that Brexit is now regarded as a failure.

Brexit is a failure, but only because Britain now has the worst of both worlds. It is outside the EU when it is inconvenient and expensive to be outside and it is within the EU when it is inconvenient and expensive to be in it.

The result is that Britain's imports from the EU are rising inexorably while exports are collapsing.

The battle of Brexit has been won by the eurocrats.

And since the remainers now control the British Government, it was always going to be thus.

Staunch remainers are still re-fighting the Brexit battle and blaming Britain's departure from the EU for all its developing woes, even though those woes (rising food and fuel prices and so on) have absolutely nothing to do with Britain's membership of the EU. The remainers would happily blame bad weather and the failure of sports teams on Brexit if they thought they could get away with it.

It now looks increasingly likely that the UK will be broken up as a result of campaigning by those seeking independence (and a return to the EU) for the three smaller, less prosperous parts of the UK.

In May 2022, Sinn Fein (campaigning for a united Ireland) won the largest number of seats in the Northern Ireland Assembly and can, therefore, nominate Northern Ireland's First Minister. It seems only a matter of time before Ireland is united again. Ireland, of course, is a member of the European Union – though the politicians there seem more enthusiastic than the voters.

Nationalist politicians in Scotland and Wales are still fighting for their countries to become independent. Ironically, many seem to want their countries to re-join the European Union. This will mean them losing their identity as individual countries and becoming part of a bureaucratic organisation which is totally opposed to national identities and which is enthusiastically supportive of social credit programmes.

Bribery

The social credit programme which is such an important part of the Great Reset is being promoted through one of the oldest tricks in the world – bribery.

Doctors are being bribed with huge fees for giving covid-19 jabs. (The fees being given are inexplicably much higher than the fees for giving more traditional vaccines.)

Journalists and their publishers were bought with hundreds of millions of pounds spent on advertising. Without government advertising, most broadcasters and publishers would have gone bankrupt and journalists would have lost their jobs.

Scientists were 'bought' when it was made clear that those who spoke out and tried to spread the truth would be demonised, silenced and fired.

Teachers were bought with long holidays on full pay when schools were closed quite unnecessarily.

Civil servants were bought by being allowed to work at home.

And the rest of the workforce was bribed with free money for staying at home and watching TV.

Cars

For years now, roads in towns and cities everywhere in Europe have been subjected to very expensive redesign work. Chicanes have been built, roads have been narrowed and large pots containing trees have been planted in the middle of thoroughfares. All this has been done without consultation, at great expense and with absolutely no sense of logic. The only consolation is that speed humps (aka sleeping policemen) have been removed (at enormous expensive) since it has been established that they are a genuine health hazard.

The areas which have been altered are known as 'low traffic neighbourhoods' and many of the people living in them have found that they can no longer get to work or visit friends or relatives without making a long detour (which, inevitably, costs a good deal in fuel or fares). The other consequence is that other neighbouring roads which aren't decorated with chicanes and potted trees are now massively busier than before as they have to take all the traffic. Just to add to the excitement, new, constantly changing speed limits have been introduced. In Wales there is talk of 20mph speed limits on all urban roads. This, of course, will lead to more accidents and (since many cars are inefficient at such a low speed) much higher fuel consumption figures.

These changes are made by collaborators working for the conspirators. When one council in London organised a debate, just under two thirds of those offering a view said that they did not like their area being turned into a low traffic neighbourhood. The Council which had asked for input from the public considered this result and responded by ignoring the public and making the changes permanent.

This, of course, is a typical 'Great Reset' way of doing things. The people who have wriggled into power pretend to be interested in the views of the people. They hold meetings. They pretend to listen. And then they do exactly what they planned to do in the first place.

New laws making motoring difficult and dangerous are being introduced almost daily. Smart motorways (proven to be dangerous and to cause long queues for no good reason whatsoever) are being built with unregulated enthusiasm. Toll roads are to be introduced and fitted with cameras and sensors which can automatically take fees from the motorist's bank account. A senior police officer has encouraged cyclists to wear helmet cameras to catch motorists breaking the Highway Code. At least two motorists have been fined for travelling faster than a cyclist felt was appropriate when they were travelling in the opposite direction. One cyclist claims to have used his helmet camera to report over 1,000 motorists to the police (this is wholesale snitching).

According to the new UK Highway Code, drivers can get into

trouble in the UK if they drive in a car which is stuffy. The punishment is two years in prison. It is also an offence to wear the wrong sort of sunglasses in sunny weather or not to wear sunglasses at all. Driving after taking hayfever medicine can result in six months in prison. And driving on wet roads after a summer shower may be regarded as a driving offence. Paying at a drive through or toll road with a mobile phone is also an offence. Not pulling in to the pavement or verge if a cyclist is approaching on the other side of the road may be an offence too. Life on the open road is such fun these days.

If motorists obey the instructions included in the Highway Code then the whole of Britain will come to a standstill.

For example, motorists must now give cyclists at least 4 foot 9 inches of space when overtaking them. That is the height of a short person. The problem is that Britain's roads mostly have lanes which are 12 feet wide. Most cars and other vehicles are between six and seven feet wide. If we assume that a cyclist will ride with his wheels three feet out from the kerb to avoid hitting pedestrians and tree trunks with his handlebars then it is clear that one cyclist on a road could hold up traffic for long periods and cause massive tailbacks. Since cars use more fuel when travelling slowly, this will lead to more pollution and greater use of fuel. If cyclists ride two abreast (as is common) then it will be impossible for a car to pass them.

As an aside it is worth remembering that cyclists pay no road tax and no insurance.

Finally, even parking a car can be extra hazardous, and intrusive, these days. Many councils have for some time demanded that motorists put their car number details into the parking machine. This is done to prevent motorists being good Samaritans and handing a partially unused ticket to another motorist but it also means that the authorities know precisely where motorists are at any time. Worse still, more and more councils are introducing special parking Apps which require the motorist to use their smart phone in order to park. The parking App is not just extremely intrusive, it is also a step towards using social credit to control motorists. If you have a poor social credit rating then you won't be allowed to park. (I wonder how legal it is to force customers to buy a smart phone in order to park a car in a public car park.)

Cash

The disappearance of cash is accelerating and is an essential step in the move towards a digital world and a globally controlled digital currency. It was one of the things I warned about in my first video 'The Coronavirus Hoax' back in March 2020.

Small towns everywhere are now without a single bank. In Britain, half of the bank branches have closed. Nearly a quarter of free to use cash machines have gone. Seven Parliamentary constituencies in the UK have seen every bank branch close. Banks used the fake threat of covid-19 (now proven to be nothing more than the rebranded flu) to accelerate closure programmes.

It is the elderly and those living in the countryside who suffer most. This is no accident, of course, for the plan is to get rid of the elderly and to force country dwellers to move into high rise apartments in large towns and cities.

Moreover, thanks to the enthusiasm of the dim-witted collaborators (many of whom are still wearing their stupid, deadly dangerous face coverings) there are now fewer shops which will take cash and it is almost impossible to buy petrol or diesel without using plastic. The collaborators love waving their little plastic cards around because they don't see where it's leading.

Children

As a result of the lockdowns, it is estimated that 90,000 children in the UK will start secondary school unable to read or write. It's reckoned that 400,000 children are now mentally ill. I believe those are massive underestimates.

These children will never ever recover. They have been destroyed by lockdowns, social distancing and masks that have all been proven not to work. Politicians don't give a damn. Scientific advisors don't give a damn. Teachers certainly don't give a damn. And too many parents don't give a damn either.

This is a war between the informed and the ignorant, the courageous and the cowardly, the dignified and the undignified, the respectful and disrespectful. Unless we win this war we are all going to die except for the evil elite.

Churches

During the last two years, you might have thought that some comfort might have been provided by the churches. Not a bit of it. In my view, the Archbishop of Canterbury and the Pope both need defrocking and locking up for they have betrayed the people they're supposed to care for.

The closure of churches and the removal of spiritual comfort at a time when people needed it most was not just unnecessary and cowardly – in my opinion it was evil. The disappearance of traditional religion was all part of the plan, of course. Check it out. See the UN's plans for Chrislam. You'll find Tony Blair mentioned. They no longer bother keeping any of it secret.

I wonder if the Archbishop of Canterbury, who seems to me to have repeatedly betrayed the people, realises he is supporting and promoting communism

Maybe he does.

After all, there is a long, strong history suggesting that the church has more in common with communism than might at first be thought.

The mediaeval church disapproved of independence, competition and self-employment. Craftsmen were forbidden by the church to improve their tools or working methods in case they gained an advantage over other workmen.

The formal Christian church regards pride as a sin, profit as a sign of greed, beauty as a path to vanity and, taking us full circle, ambition as inseparable from pride.

What is the difference between that and communism?

Clothes

Within the Great Reset, the plan is that clothes, like houses and cars, will be rented. Some clothing will be rented long-term. Some will be rented for the evening or the weekend.

Common Purpose

The UK Column has reported how a charity called Common Purpose became involved in selecting future health service managers, with the eventual development of a section within the NHS called NHS leaders – fast tracked individuals apparently destined to lead the NHS.

It seems that it is as a result of this development that the management style within the NHS became bullying and domineering, with the emphasis taken away from caring and healing and put on profits. There was, it is alleged, also a manipulation of NHS staff, using the sort of psychological tricks favoured by the Government.

The UK Column claims that Common Purpose (which is officially a charity) was funded by major banks and was given the aim of changing society – by, for example, introducing mantras and by assuming that covid patients who had not been jabbed were on a death pathway.

Cognitive dissonance among NHS staff is now so widespread that there is no discussion of the real figures about the rebranded flu, or about the jab that doesn't stop people catching covid or spreading it but does kill people.

It is because of these changes in approach that patients suffering from respiratory problems are given respiratory depressants, while advice given by hugely profitable drug companies is accepted without question or debate.

Everywhere that we look, we see psychologists controlling populations and it seems that through the organisation Common Purpose there is much control going on within the health care services of countries around the world.

This is all part of the Great Reset.

Monopolies invariably offer poor value and shoddy service. The NHS is no exception.

Communism

In a video about face coverings which was first published on 24th June 2021, I quoted someone called Susan Michie who isn't a medical doctor but who is an important advisor to the British government and director of a centre for Behaviour Change.

Comrade Michie said that we should wear face coverings forever and stick to social distancing and I wouldn't be surprised if she gets her way. This is all about control.

No one seems to care that Michie is a communist.

Can you imagine the fuss if a government advisor were a member of any organisation such as UKIP or the BNP? The BBC and The Guardian would implode.

Those who are blasé and unworried by what is happening should remember that although Lenin did not represent the Russian people and had the backing only of a tiny group of homicidal maniacs he, nevertheless, succeeded in taking control of Russia.

And Hitler rose to power with the help of a small group of followers and with finance raised from amoral and corrupt industrialists who saw the potential for huge profits. Most Germans thought Hitler and those who stood beside him were extremists. Their error was to underestimate the threat they posed. And, in many cases, to listen to, and be beguiled by, the promises.

Revolutions everywhere have always been organised in the name of the people but they have always been organised and controlled by small groups of fanatics.

If nothing is done to stop them, then before long a small group of people (Rothschild, Schwab, Gates, Musk, Obama, Prince Charles, Blair, etc.) will take control of the world. They will be aided and abetted by a bunch of deluded cultists and an army of ignorant, gutless collaborators who are more concerned with what the mainstream media tell them is 'news' than with what is really going on in the world around them.

In a communist country (and communist countries have always been run on the same principles as countries where social credit is the ruling force) the bureaucrats control the economy, the courts, the lawyers, the judges, the politics, the newspapers, the television and the radio. The bureaucrats control all societies and associations, however small and apparently unimportant they might seem to be. The privilege of working as a doctor, acting in a play or writing a book can be withdrawn without explanation.

They sometimes like to call it socialism. But it's communism. It's the Great Reset. And it's a world controlled by social credit.

And if you are wondering why billionaire conspirators should want a communist world then you haven't thought it through.

The billionaire conspirators long ago made it clear that their intention is to get rid of seven billion people – leaving just 500 million. By then the billionaire conspirators will own everything and the 500 million who are left will be their slaves, polishing the brass on their super-yachts with nary a moment of complaint.

Compassion

Compassion isn't innate in humans. It is something that has to be learned. As readers of 'Lord of the Flies' will remember, children can be horrifyingly cruel and vicious if they are not taught to behave with sensitivity and compassion.

Today, children are not being taught to be compassionate.

For example, everything that children see and hear encourages them to think of the elderly as stupid and a burden. Children are encouraged to regard other people's grandparents (and even their own) as an expensive burden for society and, therefore, for them – and, as they themselves grow a little older, to blame the elderly for their own unsatisfied financial ambitions.

This lack of compassion makes it easier for the authorities (acting on orders from the conspirators) to kill off the elderly by failing to provide them with decent medical care, by over-dosing them with benzodiazepines and morphine and by failing to provide them with essential food and water when they are in hospital.

Contactless Payments

The conspirators need us to be in debt.

If we are in debt then we are vulnerable and we can be controlled by those who control inflation and interest rates.

Contactless cards were sold to people as a convenient way to pay for things and they have proved very popular – over two thirds of all credit card transactions are conducted with contactless cards.

However, most of the people who flash their card at the reader in a shop don't even bother to look to see how much they are paying for their coffee or their ticket. Distracted and comforted by the knowledge that the transaction can't possibly cost them more than £100 they move their card across the reader without thinking.

What many probably don't realise is that the internet enables businesses to put up their prices on a minute by minute basis. Software enables companies to change their prices all the time. The prices of airline tickets change by the minute and similar software enables taxis to change their pricing all the time.

Most people who use contact cards will have no idea of the financial trouble they are in until they have accumulated serious debts.

Anyone who has accumulated credit card debts will, of course, be defenceless when social credit schemes are introduced to control debt levels. And those with debts will be considered 'bad' people.

Controlled Opposition

'Controlled opposition' describes someone who is pretending to be a truth-teller but is, in fact, paid or controlled or influenced by the conspirators.

The destruction of reputations has been so thoroughly consistent, determined and wicked that there are many who believe that any alleged truth-teller who still has accounts with YouTube, Facebook and Twitter, as well as a 'clean' Wikipedia page, is almost certainly a member of the army of frauds known as 'controlled opposition'.

Credit Rating

We've all had a credit rating or a credit score for years. The rating consists of a number (usually a three digit number) that is supposed to reflect how reliable you are at repaying money you have borrowed. Your rating is based on how you've handled money in the past and your credit rating will influence your chances of being able to borrow money to buy a house or a car, your ability to take out a contract for the supply of services such as gas and electricity, your retail credit (how likely a firm will be to give you a charge card or allow you to buy something on hire purchase), your freedom to pay bills in instalments and even your chances of being allowed to take out a mobile phone contract.

Different companies use different information and so your credit rating will vary from one company to another.

Moreover, errors can easily be made. You can get a poor rating by mistake or because you have never borrowed money and therefore not had to repay any loans. You may be a millionaire but if you have never had to repay a loan then you will probably have a poor or non-existent rating.

And you may be given a poor rating because you are married to or live with or are associated or related to someone who has a poor credit rating.

Credit ratings are very much like social credit.

Cultural Appropriation

Borrowing the culture of another race, tribe or nation is considered to be a serious social media crime and, therefore, a social credit crime. And so individuals who choose to dress in clothes usually associated with those of a different culture are likely to be subjected to trolling, abuse and complaints and possibly likely to find themselves in trouble with the law.

It is inevitable, therefore, that such behaviour will result in the loss of social credit points.

Logically (or, possibly, illogically) we have now reached the point where it is inappropriate to eat the food associated with another culture.

So, for example, it is no stretch to imagine that Caucasians who eat Indian or Chinese food will be guilty of cultural appropriation and likely to lose social credit points. And occidentals who use chopsticks when eating Chinese food can definitely expect to be accused of enhanced cultural appropriation.

Democracy

Freedom and democracy, measured around the globe, have both been shrinking for years. Once the Great Reset has arrived, and we are living under the social credit system, there will be no need at all for any sort of democracy and so freedom will be merely a memory.

Demonstrations

All around the world, governments are bringing in new laws to control the rights of the individual to demonstrate their views in opposition to the policies of their government.

For England and Wales, the UK Parliament (which also consists of Scottish members of parliament) has brought in the Police, Crime, Sentencing and Courts Bill which will give the police massively increased authority over demonstrators.

The police will in future be able to impose start and finish times on demonstrations. The police will be allowed to decide if the demonstrators are making too much noise. And the size of a demonstration is of no consequence since the new law applies to one person with a placard as much as it applies to 100,000 people with placards.

It is now a crime not to follow the law when demonstrating. Ignorance of the demands and expectations of a local police force is absolutely no defence. The police no longer have to give protestors a warning. The police can contain a crowd indefinitely (bottling them up, or 'kettling' them, in a side street, for example). And the police can effectively ignore the Human Rights Act, which gives individuals the right to make their views known.

There is no doubt that anyone who protests will lose points from their social credit rating. The wide availability of facial recognition cameras means that individuals can be identified and punished without difficulty.

Digital Currency

Nine out of ten nations are already planning to introduce central bank digital currencies which will take the place of cash. And companies are preparing to join the digital bonanza.

MasterCard has already introduced a new system allowing retailers to take payment from customers without using cash or a credit card. In May 2022, stores in Brazil were already equipped with machines which enabled them to use facial recognition and fingerprint or palm-print scanning devices to pay for goods.

MasterCard said that it intended to roll out the scheme globally before the end of 2022. The company said that customers loved the new way of paying which they described as more hygienic. They claimed that polls showed that 74% of the global population had a 'positive attitude' towards biometrics.

It was claimed that the system will be less open to fraud than other payment methods though I would doubt this very much. Crooks are usually much sharper than finance companies.

Digital currencies are the gateway to social credit.

Digital ID

When vaccine passports were introduced they were sold to the public as a way of keeping everyone safe. They were nothing to do with health, of course. The vaccine passports were merely a prelude to the much more intrusive digital ID passports.

Digital ID checks are a fundamental part of the Great Reset. The idea is to force everyone to use a smart phone App or a website in order to access anything they want to use. Eventually facial recognition and finger print scans will be used.

Citizens will need a digital ID to buy stuff, to get into places (such as shops and hospitals) and in order to access the internet. Without a digital ID you will be shut out of society.

Egged on by toxic conspirators at the World Economic Forum, governments everywhere are racing to introduce digital ID checks as quickly as possible. In Canada, Ontario and Alberta are already introducing digital ID checks, meaning that citizens will have to use a smart phone to access their bank accounts, to make medical appointments or to get married. There is no doubt that smart phones will also be needed in order to vote (though, of course, there won't be much point in voting).

And Prime Minister Trudeau in Canada has shown that bank accounts and savings aren't safe. Trudeau made the word distrain fashionable. It means that the Government has the right to steal your assets and close your bank account if you dare speak out and share the truth. (The definition of 'distrain' is to seize property in lieu of money owed. Governments are redefining the language to suit themselves.)

So, what's wrong with ID passports, the compliant will ask.

Well, there's nothing wrong with them if you don't mind the authorities knowing where you are and what you are doing every minute of every day. There is nothing wrong with them if you don't mind the authorities storing every bit of information about you (and making it available to many of your fellow citizens – quite possibly including your neighbours and relatives). There is nothing wrong with them if you are happy to accept a social credit rating which will decide whether or not your behaviour entitles you to rent a home or buy food.

Digital Shaming

It is important to remember that one of the fundamental tenets of the Great Reset is the demise of the individual. And digital shaming (done by largely anonymous trolls, often orchestrated by sponsored ringleaders) is a fundamental weapon in the destruction of the individual.

Anyone who expresses views which do not fit in with the official line, is likely to find themselves vilified and exiled. The shaming isn't perhaps quite as physically brutal as the wooden stocks which were such a popular part of English life not many centuries ago, but the aim (to silence dissent by embarrassment, shame and mental torment) is destructive and effective.

Trolling is the internet equivalent of the poison pen letter or the scribbled, abusive graffiti scrawled on a wall.

During the earliest and most aggressive days of 2020, people who were known to have travelled were publicly shamed not just by friends and neighbours but also by governments. The Vietnamese government, which is said to use newspaper leaks to frighten its citizens, or to persuade them to do 'what is regarded as 'the right thing', invited the press to watch a live stream of a meeting about one young woman's medical condition. She had (or was alleged to have) the rebranded flu. In less than a day the patient's Instagram account had received ten thousand new followers with many of them attacking her. The patient was still in a hospital bed but many of those postings claimed to have seen her out and about in public 'infecting passers-by'.

The Vietnamese government stirred up more controversy and in the UK, the Daily Mail (which was once a newspaper but is now a propaganda sheet for governments around the world) claimed, without any evidence, that the woman was a 'super spreader'.

The Vietnamese government upped the ante still further and posted photos of the woman recovering in hospital. This made things worse. Trolls dug up old pictures of her and wrote abusive comments.

Still, the Vietnamese woman (whom I have deliberately not named) got off fairly lightly compared to those doctors who dared to tell the truth during 2020 and onwards. I speak with experience.

Disinformation and Misinformation

The world is now very much controlled by a large army of fact checkers, misinformation experts and disinformation experts. Most of these people seem to have absolutely no qualifications of any kind and certainly none that might be considered appropriate.

In the UK, the Online Harms Act demands that platforms censor content or face fines and/or jail time. The Government in the UK can already force social media companies to remove anything the State authorities deem unacceptable (it doesn't have to be untrue for them to consider it unacceptable, just unacceptable). Criticism of vaccines or vaccine programmes is always considered unacceptable.

When Elon Musk first talked about buying Twitter and dared to mention the phrase 'freedom of speech', the UK Prime Minister Boris Johnson quickly warned that Musk would have to keep Twitter 'accountable' in terms of 'content material restrictions'.

In the early summer of 2022, the US Department of Homeland Security (which was set up after the events of the 9th of September 2001 – which I described at the time as a false flag event and which no doubt helped set in motion the events which are currently threatening us all) has set up a Disinformation Governance Board to decide what information is truthful and what isn't. Like most similar organisations it appears to be very left wing in bias.

The official line seems to be that free speech is a bad thing and that freethinkers and truth-tellers must be controlled by legislation.

US President Biden ordered the US Surgeon General to tell Big Tech to turn over the details of anyone who has spread misinformation about covid on the internet. I was thrilled when I first heard this. I assumed it meant that the US Surgeon General would be demanding that Big Tech hand over the names of all those mainstream journalists who have been spreading misinformation. But I was wrong, of course. What Biden really meant was that Big

Tech had to hand over details of all independent-minded, intelligent, well-informed citizens who've told the truth. This is another step in the censorship and demonization of the truth-tellers.

DNA

In June 2020 I warned that the PCR tests could and would be used to collect DNA samples. (After all the polymerase chain reaction procedures – PCR tests to you and I – were originally designed – years ago – to collect DNA samples.)

It became clear in 2021 that the PCR test was, indeed, being used to collect DNA samples, without the knowledge or consent of millions of individuals, and that the samples were being sold to whoever wanted to buy them – and could afford them.

Just how the DNA samples will be used is still unknown but it seems a fair bet that the information will be used as part of the Great Reset and the social credit system.

Economy

The destruction of the economy, through the sanctions against Russia, the absurd 'long covid' (being used by millions as an excuse to stay away from work) the massive debts built up as a result of the multi-billion pound frauds of 2020 and 2021, and the wicked nonsense of the global warming fraud is going to lead to a massive worldwide recession – far bigger than the recession of the 1930s. Even the World Bank, not an organisation which I regard very highly, has warned that the Ukraine war and sanctions will slow growth and increase poverty.

It's all deliberate, of course. Millions of people will lose their jobs and never work again. Last year alone, 17,000 chain store shops closed in the UK and will never reopen. The basic income scheme already being trialled in Wales will spread, and the middle and working classes will disappear to be replaced by armies of forgotten and put upon drones. World trade and globalisation will soon be a thing of the past. The UK will suffer more than most countries.

As a result of lockdowns, sanctions, zero carbon policies and other government actions, prices are soaring and they'll keep going up.

The British Chancellor, Rishi Sunak, who gets my prize as one of the most disreputable men in Britain, has done more than his bit to win a seat on the world government.

In the UK, as a result of government policies, mortgage rates are rising, petrol retailers are profiteering and household energy prices are soaring beyond comprehension. The figures show that food inflation rose over 5% last month, holidays and travel will soon be no more than a memory, clothing and shoes went up 8.8% and pub and restaurant prices will soon be beyond people who are not called Sunak and who do not enjoy the financial delights of a rich father-in-law and lots of clever advice on cutting the family tax bill. Council taxes are rising as fast as services are deteriorating, train prices will average a 9.8% rise this year, postage stamps went up over 10%, furniture is up 9.2% and subscriptions everywhere are rocketing.

They're talking about rationing in Germany and if you're not in Germany they'll be talking about it round your way soon. Factories are going to close. Street lights will go off. Meanwhile, as MPs enjoy massive pay rises, we pensioners are denied the pay rise we were promised by the Government. Sunak is more dangerous to pensioners than midazolam.

And anyone who hoped to supplement their miserable state pension with their own investments or pension fund will be unlucky. The people who control big investment and pension companies, with over $22 trillion in assets, are making decisions based not on investment logic but on their own moral values. So, they are selling (or refusing to invest in) companies which they consider to be in some way unethical – for example, oil companies or mining companies. And they won't even invest in companies which sell petrol. This nonsense isn't confined to so-called ethical investment funds. Massively overpaid investment managers are steadfastly destroying pensions and investments and helping to impoverish everyone except themselves.

Is this all a big coincidence? Is it just bad luck that central bankers all around the world are making the same mistakes at the same time? Is it because they are all stupid and incompetent? There isn't a central banker in the world who could pass O level sums and if any of them designed a drinking mug they'd put the handle on the inside and leave a hole in the bottom to aid cooling.

But I don't think it is all a coincidence, or a result of incompetence.

I think the central bankers are merely working towards the Great Reset.

The total global debt was recently put at $244 trillion – three times the sum of all the money in the world which is approximately $80 trillion.

There are approximately 7.5 billion people in the world so each person has, on average, $10,600 in wealth and $21,000 in debt.

We will own less than nothing.

Education

The events of 2020, 2021 and 2022 have shown us that the majority of people lack the capacity for original thought, are too lazy to think for themselves and are frightened to 'think outside the box'.

If you find that triple example of tautology annoying then that's fine: because the premise is a crucial one. And repetition, as Gertrude Stein would doubtless agree, is essential if you wish to make a point.

Most citizens are now led by knee jerk reflexes – responding, unquestioningly, to what they see and hear on television. They believe nonsense such as 'climate change is scary', 'covid is dangerous' and 'vaccines are good' because they see and hear these thoughts repeated all day long.

They do not understand that what they are hearing has been devised by the conspirators, deliberately created to produce fear and confusion, and spread by the collaborators.

But, why are people so ready to believe what they hear and to accept it unquestioningly?

The answer is that the modern education system (both in school and university) discourages and actually suppresses original thought and debate. Thinking parents spend much of their time struggling to un-teach the propaganda that has been drilled into their children's minds.

Teachers today seem unaware that it takes more effort to reject an idea than to accept it. Acceptance is something we do without thinking but rejecting something which we are told requires effort.

However, instead of encouraging students to question what they are told, teachers simply instruct their students to accept the 'official' view. Teachers and university lecturers worry endlessly about the 'sin' of unconscious bias but seem unaware of their own conscious bias.

Descartes believed that after preliminarily accepting an idea, we then think about it and decide whether to reject it or not. But, a good few years later, Baron Spinoza suggested that when we accept an idea, we think we understand it and so we no longer question it. As usual Descartes was wrong. And in this, at least, Spinoza was right.

The problem today is that people are prone to accept the things they see or hear – on television or the radio or the classroom, and it is formal teaching which pushes students into blindly, unquestioningly, uncritically accepting whatever they're told in later life. (There goes that triple tautology again.)

The mainstream media now exists to flood us with information which reinforces existing beliefs. And the journalists, commentators and conspirators know that rejecting existing beliefs requires energy and effort so we are bombarded with false and misleading information which supports the false and misleading ideas we have been given.

Teachers and lecturers have, for decades now, failed to explain to students that unbelieving things we have been fed is an essential part of wisdom and, more fundamentally, an essential part of growing up and developing 'a mind of our own'.

We are all overwhelmed with information but teachers have not taught students how to deal with that overload. Most students remain unquestioning because it is easy and convenient. And, particularly now that much grading is done by teachers who have the power to assess their own students, it is the simple route to better grades.

So students merely accept what they are told. And when they grow up they still accept what they are told.

And so the unthinking masses accept the frauds of the Great Reset and the New World Order.

Today, the result is that only the intelligent and free-thinking question the Great Reset and the confines of social credit.

Teachers and lecturers must take a big chunk of the blame for failing to teach their students how to think or, rather, how not to think.

Our educational system, like our health care system, is unfit for purpose.

As a result, literacy and numeracy levels are at an all-time low among teenagers. Most school leavers cannot add up without a calculator and cannot read or write their own language fluently.

School teachers, seemingly led and controlled by militant, over-zealous trade unions, cooperated in destroying the nation's education system by closing schools unnecessarily and by insisting that children be damaged with deadly and useless masks. The incidence of serious mental health problems among children of all ages is also at an all-time high. If you think this is all still a coincidence, then keep taking those tablets. If they're lucky the children referred for mental health care might get an appointment to see someone in 10 or 15 years' time. And I hope you don't think I'm kidding.

An official OFSTED report exposed how the covid-19 policy had devastated children's lives and hindered their development.

Teachers, along with doctors, social workers and politicians should be arrested. But no one will be punished. We live according to Schwab's rules now.

In Wales, in 2023, students will again receive advance information about the content of the tests they will be expected to take. (Translated into English this means that they will be allowed to see their exam papers in advance. Only the very dimmest pupils will fail to obtain full marks.) This is all part of the plan to destroy education and make children more pliable, more compliant and less likely to think for themselves.

Schools everywhere close on the flimsiest of pretexts. If there is a slight breeze then all schools will shut in case a child is injured by a flying leaf. After a boy was injured at school, the council announced that 'all campuses…will be closed…on health and safety grounds. Learners will access blended learning.' I had to use a search engine to find out what 'blended learning' is. Apparently, it really just means online learning. It's a tragedy that the boy was injured. But if you shut campuses every time someone is injured then every school will be pretty well permanently shut. But then that's the idea isn't it?

Teachers are too dumb to realise that they will be entirely replaced by blended learning. When the only teaching is done via the internet, the authorities will need only one teacher for each subject. All the rest will be fired. (The same thing is true for doctors who refuse to see patients any more. They will be replaced by computers – who have been proven to be better at making diagnoses and performing surgery. And the computers can probably be programmed to be kind and friendly too.

The aim, of course, is to produce future generations who are illiterate, innumerate and unable to think for themselves. Children are indoctrinated by teachers who have themselves been misinformed and indoctrinated.

Millions are being trained to be indifferent to suffering and reliably compliant – always ready to do as they are told and to be turned into collaborators, supporting the ever-powerful conspirators.

They will be the ever-patient, collaborating drones in a world controlled by a World Government and a conspiracy of billionaires.

Extremism

The word extremism has been co-opted as a synonym for terrorism and anyone classified as a terrorist or an extremist will fare very badly under any social credit scheme.

In the UK, the Government has launched a 'call for evidence to understand people's experience of extremism and its impact on social cohesion'.

Dame Sara Klaus, the Government's Independent Advisor for Social Cohesion and Resilience (I particularly like the word 'independent' when it appears in a title for a Government appointed anyone) called for evidence from those who have been targeted by extremists.

So, what is an extremist? And who decides who is an extremist?

Well, in the United States, it has been decided that anyone who is opposed to covid measures is top of the list for extremists.

And back in the UK there is a Commission for Countering Extremism which has produced a report which concluded: 'The covid-19 pandemic has provided a breeding ground for conspiracy theories, disinformation and hateful extremism.'

So, anyone questioning the official line about covid-19 is officially spreading false information and conspiracy theories. And anyone encouraging people to research and question what they have been told is a dangerous extremist.

Fact Checking the Fact Checkers

I usually ignore the fact checkers because the whole fact checking business is a well remunerated farce. I've been fact checked hundreds of times and although they have huffed and puffed a good deal (and lied a good deal more) they have not found one error in any of my books, videos or articles.

Thousands of greedy nerds with laptops have set up fact checking sites and obtained huge sums of money from organisations desperate to defend their lies.

Many of the fact checkers get some, most or all of their money from Facebook, Google, YouTube and the Bill and Melinda Gates Foundation, and it is not surprising, therefore, that I have never yet seen a fact checker who finds against a government or drug company. They rarely or never check any facts, they rarely if ever check with the people they're criticising and they often, usually or always know their conclusion before they start. The fact checkers are, like the BBC and the rest of the mainstream media, misinformation specialists – that is to say, they specialise in spreading misinformation.

However, because fact checkers are forcing themselves into the public eye, I looked at three who published material about me in the days after my video about heart problems and the jabs (published on BrandNewTube on 22nd November 2021 and entitled 'Finally! Medical Proof the (rebranded flu) Jab is 'Murder').

First, there is a website called Lead Stories which claims to be a Facebook third party fact checking partner and a member of something called the Coronavirus Facts Alliance. Their top two main funding sources for 2020 were Facebook and Google and something called ByteDance. They also receive money from Coronavirus Facts Alliance. They admit, however, that the bulk of their revenue comes from Facebook.

Who are these organisations? Well, the Coronavirus Facts Alliance is run by something which calls itself 'the international fact checking network' (IFCN) at the Poynter Institute in the USA, and this works through the Craig Newmark Center for Ethics and Leadership which was made possible by a generous grant from Craig Newmark Philanthropies. Craig Newmark is the bloke who set up Craigslist. This seems to me to be a very pointy pyramid.

ByteDance is a Chinese internet tech company headquartered in Beijing and domiciled in the Cayman Islands. I can tell you no more.

The writer of the piece at Lead Stories was not, as you might hope, a professor of cardiology or even a doctor or even a nurse but a woman called Alexis Tereszcuk who spent over a decade breaking hard news and celebrity scoop with something called radaronline and a magazine called US Weekly. As the entertainment editor, she investigated Hollywood stories and conducted interviews with A list celebrities and reality stars. She is apparently known for her work on 'The Gossip Queens' and 'Most Shocking Reality TV Moments'.

Alexis says that the abstract I quoted in my video does not make claims of death from the covid vaccine nor does it assert that covid vaccines should be halted. True. I interpreted and commented on the evidence. That's what I do and what I've been doing for over 50 weary years.

She then goes on to say, referring to the paper I quoted, that 'their preliminary experiment shows an increase in endothelial inflammatory markers'.

The key word here is experiment.

And the point that she perhaps doesn't understand – despite that background of interviewing reality TV stars and celebrities – is that when serious problems appear with an experiment you should look seriously and if there is also evidence of deaths then you stop the experiment.

This same woman also previously criticised a video in which I proved conclusively that the rebranded flu has a mortality rate similar to the usual flu.

As proof for her assertion she says that the number who died in the US from covid-19 was 594,000 as of May 31st 2021 which is almost 10 times as many as died in the 2017-8 flu season.

Now this is utterly bizarre.

First, I suspect, she may have mixed the word 'from' with the word 'with'. Both are four letter words so that's understandable.

Second, she is comparing lemons to sandals. I wrote about UK figures. She's using US figures.

Third, the figure of 594,000, is generally recognised as being a massive exaggeration because of the habit of putting people down as dying from covid when they also had co-morbidities.

Fourth, she is comparing the total from the end of 2019 to the end of May 2021 – that's nearly 18 months and she's comparing it with a six month flu season which she selected.

Fifth, why pick the figures for 2017-18?

Maybe Alexis should go back to writing about minor royals and reality television. But maybe Facebook pays better.

Next there is something called Logically which says it is a technology company with one of the world's largest dedicated fact checking teams. But then, to paraphrase Mandy Rice Davies 'they would say that wouldn't they'.

The majority shareholder of Logically is someone called Lyric Jain who is 25-years-old and describes himself as a serial entrepreneur. Logically also secured funding from Massachusetts Institute of Technology through an investment grant which supports student founded businesses.

Mr Jain is the only person with significant control of Logically. He says he used his own boot-strapped savings, whatever that is, private equity money and money from the fairly small family business of Eliza Tinsley which sells fencing, ropes, gate fittings and straps and ties.

Logically is variously said to have 90, 70 or 25 fact checkers and several in house journalists. I couldn't really confirm any of that. The fact checking team was said to be in India. It's difficult to find.

Logically describes me as 'a noted spreader of health misinformation' – which is about as libellous as you can get, and complains that the abstract which I quoted contains several typographical errors. Wow. If I thought Lyric had enough money to make it worthwhile I'd sue them. I'd win but my fear is that I might end up with a huge legal bill.

Logically complains that the sample size of 566 people in the paper is extremely small. This will come as a big surprise to drug companies. I've seen studies published on a hundredth of that. I've seen drugs put on the market with no human experimentation at all – just animals.

The report was written by Ernie. No idea of name or qualifications. There is no list of writers or their backgrounds. Ernie might be a giraffe for all I know.

Ernie the fact checker has also written a fact checking report attacking the idea that people wearing face masks breathe in more carbon dioxide.

His or her evidence is that CO_2 molecules are much smaller than the holes in masks and so the CO_2 goes through easily.

This seems to me to be a really stupid argument because the face covering material is clearly still preventing most of the airflow.

That seems to be it for Ernie.

He doesn't quote any scientific papers – I have published scores of scientific references he could have looked at. And he doesn't seem to be aware of the scientific evidence showing that those who wear face coverings end up with high carbon dioxide levels – and low oxygen levels.

The truth, of course, is that masks do more harm than good. Even Dr Fauci and Dr Whitty agreed that the darned things are no more than virtue signalling.

Ernie's 0 out of 10 attempt at fact checking is merely helping to sustain the Government's lies.

Logically has an office in London at 12 Soho Square which is apparently one of those buildings where you can rent offices by the square foot. I checked out the building but couldn't find any mention of Logically but I'm sure they are there somewhere.

A third fact checker I saw is called Institute for Strategic Dialogue which has a headline entitled 'How Facebook's failure to remove false content allows covid-19 misinformation to spread'.

This report was written by Aoife Gallagher who was a journalist with the online news agency Storyul and has completed an MA in journalism from TU Dublin. TU Dublin is Technological University Dublin. She seems from her posts to have a pro-vaccine outlook but, hey, I could be wrong.

Aoife studied the World Doctors Alliance on Facebook and words like false information appeared. The WDA is an organisation of which I am a member – it is a group of several thousand medical people probably infinitely more qualified than all the world's fact checkers put together.

WDA apparently has 550,000 followers on Facebook, and I'm guessing Aoife thinks this is a bad thing. But if she does have a pro-vaccine outlook perhaps that isn't the best starting point for an independent fact checker.

Now ISD grew out of the Club of Three and they have a list of funders.

And the top name on the list – which may be alphabetical and probably is – is the Bill and Melinda Gates Foundation.

ISD also receive money from Facebook, Google and Microsoft and YouTube, the UK Home Office, the US state department and the United Nations.

Just how you can claim to be an independent fact checker when your income comes from people like that is a mystery to me.

There's one thing that I found odd.

ISD has a graph of followers of Facebook pages associated with the World Doctors Alliance to show the influence the WDA and its followers have.

And I am number six on the list

Which is odd, and a bit of a mystery to me, because I don't have a Facebook page. Indeed, I've never even been on Facebook. Facebook banned me from joining in the spring of 2020 saying that I was a threat to their community, though just what sort of a threat they considered me to be they didn't say.

In the UK, the Government has provided taxpayers with a fact checking service to help them decide whether something is disinformation or true. Citizens, who are in doubt or confused, are advised to consult the UK Government's own website or an officially approved fact-checking service which receives financial support from Facebook and Google.

The idea of the Government providing a fact checker to help the public decide whether or not the Government has lied would be comical if it were not so serious.

Fake News

I believe the BBC is perhaps the best-known and most dangerous distributor of fake news and misinformation. By now, in a decent world, the BBC should have lost its charter and the right to claim a licence fee.

The media fraud in support of the jabs is everywhere.

For example, something called Yahoo News had a headline which read: 'Anti-vax Olympic gold medallist dies of covid aged 51.'

Anyone who read the story will have found that the unfortunate man died of covid and had been jabbed. He'd previously expressed anti-vax views but he'd been jabbed and he nevertheless died of covid.

Farmers

Traditional farmers (the ones with muddy boots, tractors and fields full of crops and animals) are constantly complaining that their lives have become impossible in recent years.

All the new regulations which are introduced make it increasingly difficult for them to make a living out of growing food. Jeremy Clarkson, a television personality who started a farm and who had no experience of farming when he began, has expressed his dismay at how planning regulations have made life difficult. He says that other farmers in the UK have reported that they also find themselves facing insuperable problems when trying to deal with planning authorities.

More remarkably, farmers are now being paid to stop farming. This is, doubtless, a development of the 'setaside' process which allowed farmers to do nothing whatsoever with some of their land but to receive payment from the European Union for doing so. (This was and is so stupid that it had to have a hidden agenda. Britain produces less than half the food it needs and has to import the rest, often at ruinous prices. There is plenty of land in the world to grow as many crops as we need. But much land is left fallow for political reasons.)

Now, the EU's apparently barmy scheme is being developed. According to the International Monetary Fund farmers are being bribed to retire and to allow their cultivated land to go wild.

The same things are happening everywhere around the world.

A shortage of animal feed means that livestock are being culled throughout Europe. In the UK cows are being exterminated because of a lack of farmworkers. Around the world, hundreds of millions of animals are being slaughtered. In the Netherlands, politicians are contemplating introducing a meat tax (to reduce meat consumption) as a contribution to the net zero campaign.

And of course, huge areas of fertile land are being covered with solar panels or wind turbines.

If they understood the aims of those promoting the Great Reset, the farmers would understand that what is happening to them is not accidental or bad luck – it is deliberate. These days very little happens that is accidental. Almost everything is part of the Big Plan for our future. The aim is for farm grown food to be replaced by food manufactured and prepared in laboratories and factories. The re-wilding process, which involves turning huge areas of farmland back into wild country, populated by wolves, bears and so on, is part of this process.

It is for the same reason that many of those with market gardens, allotments and vegetable plots in their garden are being closed down. New laws are being brought in (usually in the guise of protecting the community from infection) to stop people growing their own vegetables or keeping a few chickens. Indeed, chickens have been declared illegal animals in some parts of the world – allegedly because of the risk of bird flu, diagnosed by the totally discredited PCR test.

Again, it is vital to remember that none of this is accidental.

The plan is to get rid of farms, market gardens and private vegetable plots.

Why?

Well, it is ostensibly part of the re-wilding process (being organised all over the world) which is sold to us as a way of helping to combat global warming. But, as usual, it's all about control and giving extra power to those controlling the Great Reset.

Bill Gates has invested in major meat-substitute companies which are producing synthetic burgers, sausages and so on.

When those in charge are also in control of making, selling and distributing all the food they will be able to control who is allowed to buy food and who isn't allowed to buy food.

And that, of course, is the basic principle of the social credit system.

If you decide who gets to eat and who doesn't get to eat then you can easily control people's behaviour.

And, of course, the ultimate aim is to close the countryside to humans and to force country dwellers into tightly packed blocks of flats in smart cities where there will be very little greenery and where most people will see little of the sun and nothing of wildlife.

Fear

The conspirators create fear through catastrophe (a disease, global warming, a war) because they know that the fearful are more likely to accept authority and put up with surveillance. Frightened individuals are slow to learn, slow to protest, slow to complain and quick to comply. The truly fearful abandon their freedom and independence in return for leadership.

Governments around the world have, for years, been deliberately creating fears.

In 2020, they stepped up their fear-making and hired specialists so that they could do it more efficiently. They created hopes to match the fears and then dashed the hopes and created new fears – building them on a foundation of lies and deceits. In every country, the politicians, the scientific advisors, the TV doctors and the journalists were all part of the great fear making conspiracy.

Food

The 'designer' war that the conspirators arranged to be fought in Ukraine is going according to plan: the main aim of this war is to bring about the deaths of hundreds of millions in Africa and Asia.

Within weeks of the war starting, around 70 countries were either officially facing a critical food emergency or already in a catastrophic situation. Those 20 countries are heading for serious starvation and mass deaths.

The World Food Price index has reached a record high (and is worse than it was in the 1970s when there was a global commodities crisis). Within weeks the prices of essential foods had gone up by 23% and were still rising.

Countries which had enough food were locking their cupboards to protect their own supplies. Indonesia prohibited palm oil shipments for a while and India banned exports of wheat.

When Biden, Johnson and the other conspirators used NATO to initiate the invasion of Ukraine, they knew that Ukraine usually supplied 17% of the world's corn, 15% of the world's barley and 11% of the world's traded wheat.

They also knew that nearly half of the world's sunflower and safflower seeds come from Ukraine. (That's why vegetable oils are now rationed in the UK, France and other countries.)

When Biden, Johnson and co pushed Russia into invading Ukraine and then made things infinitely worse by introducing their genocidal sanctions policy, they knew that Russia and Ukraine provided the world with 12% of all the essential calories.

Just how many people are going to die as a result this year?

The short answer is a lot.

When this madness began there were already 161 million people living on the edge of starvation. There is no doubt that hundreds of millions will die because of the sanctions against Russia.

And there's a twist around the corner.

I expect the shortage of fuel (deliberately created by the sanctions) to be made worse as 'developed' countries turned food crops into fuel for their vehicles.

Will this make a difference?

You bet it will.

A single motor car is likely to need vast quantities of biofuel – enough of the stuff that would, if kept as food, would keep a human being alive for a year.

Meanwhile, by May 2022, food rationing had already been introduced in Spain and Germany and some items were rationed in the UK.

Food prices will continue to rise for the foreseeable future – aided to some extent by modern technology.

Five years or so ago I remember noticing that price labels on the shelves in a supermarket in Paris weren't the ordinary shelf labels but looked like the dials of rows of digital watches. The manager explained that the prices of all the goods in his shop were controlled and adjusted from the supermarket's head office.

Prices of beans, jam and mustard could be changed instantaneously in hundreds of stores by a couple of flicks of a keyboard. And prices could be changed scores of time in an hour.

Food prices rarely, if ever, go down.

Free Speech

Governments and commentators talk loudly and often about the importance of free speech. Politicians and journalists like to point to China and Russia as examples of countries where citizens are not allowed to express their views. But those of us living in the West have no free speech. For several years now the mainstream media has suppressed facts as well as opinions. This censorship suddenly got a great deal worse in the early spring of 2020.

Today, the only people who are allowed access to the media are the people who are following the official line. Anyone who complains about the lack of free speech and about the problem of police violence at demonstrations, is likely to be beaten over the head with a stick and thrown into a prison cell. The police will hold their prisoner there for 24 hours for the unofficial crime of impertinence.

After a tennis club in Wimbledon in London announced that it would ban Russian players from taking part in its Grand Slam tournament (because their home country had invaded Ukraine) other players from around the world, announced that they did not approve of the ban and called for the Wimbledon tournament to be removed from the year's list of point scoring competition.

The result was instantaneous.

The mainstream media supported the club's ban, and sports administrators and journalists quickly attacked the sympathetic players for supporting their colleagues, suggesting that if they wanted to allow the Russian players into the tournament then 'they must want to side with Putin and Russia in the invasion of Ukraine'.

Letter writing members of the public quickly joined in with more abuse. The media I saw contained no opposition to the tennis club's decision and no support for the dissenting players.

To make things worse, free speech on the internet is closed down when payment companies close the accounts of sites considered dangerous.

Peter Thiel, the German-American billionaire tech investor and co-founder of PayPal, has in the past (according to New Yorker magazine) argued that modern life is much too convoluted for truly democratic participation. The company he helped found, PayPal, has been clamping down on truth-telling websites using their payment process to raise money. The publisher of my book 'Covid-19: The Greatest Hoax in History' lost his PayPal account within hours of the book's publication. Nothing in the book is inaccurate. The publisher then immediately lost another payment account. (Thiel is on the board of directors of Facebook. His work in data analysis is reported to have been backed by the Central Intelligence Agency and he said to be a member of the Steering Committee of the Bilderberg group.)

What sort of people are they, the people who so readily demonise and abuse those telling the truth and who work so hard to suppress free speech and to destroy the lives of those who tell the truth?

Most of the editors on Wikipedia, the fake encyclopaedia, are anonymous, too cowardly to give their own names. They lie without apparent embarrassment.

A journalist for the Daily Mail said I was pretending to be a doctor which was absurd since I had worked for the Daily Mail as a doctor. The Royal Society of Arts expelled me because I had been attacked by the BBC's Panorama programme (without being given the chance to tell the truth on the programme). That was like punishing someone because they had been mugged.

Google and YouTube hide behind corporate anonymity. Over 100 of my videos were censored and deleted by YouTube even though the cowardly, anonymous editors there must have known that everything I'd said was completely accurate. They didn't even pretend they'd found any errors. Eventually, they tired of taking down honest videos and banished my channel completely, finally and permanently. Feeling that wasn't enough, they banned me from accessing the YouTube channel.

Gas-lighting

Gas-lighting is a method of encouraging people to believe lies and distrust the truth. It is a technique most commonly used by governments which spread misinformation and disinformation and yet discredit the truth and those who try to share it. Google, Wikipedia and YouTube are specialists at Gas-lighting.

Genetic Engineering

The UK Government has announced that it will change the rules on gene editing (changing the existing DNA of plants and animals).

In the past genetic engineering was ruled by legislation which matched laws introduced in 2018 under a European Court of Justice ruling. The UK Government's new ruling is designed to make research and development easier and in due course genetically edited food (both plant and animal) will be sold in the UK.

To my surprise, the farmer's union welcomed the change. A farmers' representative said that 'gene editing is about speeding up the genetic-selection process that could have occurred naturally. As we look at tackling the challenges of climate change and feeding an ever-growing population, we need all the tools available.'

That, of course, was all nonsense.

Our world is being changed fundamentally, and without any idea of where the changes will take us, in order to help us tackle the entirely spurious, pseudo-scientific nonsense that started life as global warming, morphed into climate change, has gone through several other iterations and has ended up as Net Zero – the bizarre idea that we can eradicate the use of all fossil fuels while still providing a world population in excess of seven billion people with all the food and energy they need.

The enthusiasts who have welcomed giving more authority and power to the genetic engineers believe (for no good reason that I can discern) that genetic engineering will produce healthier food. There is also an assumption (based on little more than hubris and hope) that the genetically engineered products will be resistant to weather changes and disease.

There seems to be no understanding that genetic engineering will result in a narrowing of the diversity of plants and animals. A disease which affects a widely used genetically engineered product could lead to a famine that would make the Irish potato famine look insignificant.

All the fears about genetic engineering which I expressed back in 1994 (in my book 'Food for Thought') still remain.

Back then I argued that those promoting the values of genetic engineering should be obliged to prove that their efforts would be entirely safe. The response then (and I strongly suspect it would be the response now) was that it was up to me to prove that genetically engineered products were dangerous.

This, of course, is a complete reversal of common sense and the scientific process.

What sort of monstrosities will the genetic engineers produce? What sort of hideous hybrid animals will result? How many billion will die when widely farmed genetically engineered crops fail?

If you change the natural genetic composition of a potato is it a potato? If you change the natural genetic composition of a pig is it a pig? If you change the natural genetic composition of a human is it still a human? How long before altered humans are patented – in the way that a company called Monsanto has patented seeds that have been used for hundreds of years.

No one knows the answers to these questions because the UK Government has authorized another massive experiment.

We will be the guinea pigs.

I suspect that, as a result, billions will die.

But then, that's the plan, isn't it?

Global Slavery

I've been warning for some time that the bad things that are happening were planned in the 1960s.

Today, those who aren't jabbed are already being denied medical care. Social credit schemes are being introduced everywhere – with the vax passports as the key.

But it's what comes next that is worrying me. And their plans are now all quite clear.

The climate change hoax that was planned back in the 1960s is the really big threat we are facing.

Covid-19 was the warm-up act for the big one – the global warming fraud. That was always going to be the excuse for tough new legislation, economic destruction, more genocide, the end of medical care and the introduction of the digital passports. Now, it's all coming very, very fast. And the predictable clamp downs are coming quickly too. The economy is going to be further destroyed. And truth-tellers are going to be further suppressed by the conspirators.

The conspirators at the BBC, who regard global warming as scientific fact, report that a small army of volunteers is keeping truth-telling 'deniers' off Wikipedia (in my view already the most dangerous, dishonest and corrupt website in history).

So much for freedom of speech and debate – yet again. These people are suppressing views they disagree with and the BBC treats them as dedicated heroes.

Those of us daring to tell the truth are now being targeted by counter terrorism officers on the grounds that we are undermining national health security. I first warned about the side effects associated with the mRNA jabs in a video in December 2020 when I warned that the jabs would cause deaths and illnesses including myocarditis and strokes. The warning was largely ignored and I was even further suppressed.

(Exactly the same thing happened with anti-vivisection campaigns several decades ago. My phones were tapped and I couldn't go out of doors without being followed by an officer from

Special Branch with a video camera. People scoff and no one believes it until it happens to them.)

UK Prime Minister Boris Johnson is introducing more wicked net zero legislation that will impoverish us all.

By the end of 2022, the average family will be at least 25% poorer.

The World Health Organisation is planning global laws to manage the world in the future. They'll be joining up with Schwab and the World Economic Forum. All these people are unelected, of course.

Incidentally, it's no coincidence that every leader in the world is now hated. The conspirators want us to hate our national governments so they can set the world up for a global government run by global warming cultists. The mainstream media particularly the BBC and The Guardian, both of which have financial links to Bill Gates – who appears to be regarded by the WHO as a member state – will doubtless approve the idea.

I am not exaggerating when I warn you that we are heading rapidly towards global slavery.

Remember that the United Nations member states agreed in 2019 – on April 1st no less – to implement their plans on population and development.

The plans included massive controls on population growth.

Hundreds of millions will die in Asia and Africa. The elderly and the sick will be killed. The conspirators want total control over people and events. This is democide.

In the UK, a great deal of new legislation is being pushed through to build a communist state on the back of a disease which I've proved has killed fewer people than the flu would have done in an average year.

Digital identity document validation technology (IDVT) was introduced on 6th April 2022 to 'help' employers and landlords check up on us all. Digital passports and wearable monitors will track your weight if you've been ordered to lose weight.

All these things are happening all around the world.

The conspirators are pushing through legislation on the backs of the rebranded flu – legislation designed to remove cash, introduce digital passports and take total control of every aspect of our lives.

Global Warming

Global warming (or climate change) is known to be a fraud with all the scientific validity offered by the nice bloke who used to walk up and down Oxford Street in central London, carrying a placard predicting the end of the world. There is no scientific evidence for its existence. The whole scam is built on fantasy fears, non-existent science, exaggerated predictions pulled out of thin air and predicated upon the idea that carbon dioxide is bad for the planet. Since plants depend upon carbon dioxide this is rather difficult to understand. (The enthusiasm of global warming cultists for chopping down trees makes the notion even more incomprehensible.)

Global warming was deliberately created as a weapon of control and it has been promoted and marketed as a weapon for the Great Reset.

An army of prominent scientists sent a letter to the UN Secretary general pointing out that there was no climate emergency. They were ignored. Instead, a young Swedish girl was, and is, regarded by the media as the only reliable source of information.

I dealt with global warming in my book 'A Bigger Problem than Climate Change' and those who are still unconvinced that man-made climate change is a myth should read Zina Cohen's small book 'Greta's Homework' which is packed with evidence destroying the global warming myth.

Despite the facts proving that there is no man-made global warming, questioning the myth is already forbidden. The mainstream media does not allow any debate or discussion about global warming. The BBC, for example, has decided that global warming, like vaccination, is a taboo subject. Scientists who tell the truth are demonised, suppressed or simply ignored.

Once a fully organised social credit system has been installed, anyone who questions the global warming myth will lose points and probably be banned from buying food or renting accommodation.

Insane global warming cultists, sanctimonious and ignorant, are demanding an end to all carbon emissions by 2025 and a stop to the use of all fossil fuels by that date. The result will be the deaths of hundreds of millions from starvation and cold.

The loony cultists demand that fossil fuels are replaced with hydrogen – which is made with the aid of fossil fuels; to get rid of petrol and diesel cars and replace them with electric cars which are worse for the environment, and which use electricity created with oil and gas and trees chopped up into pellets, imported and burnt instead of coal.

The cultists probably do not understand that their actions are orchestrated by the conspirators whose aims they are aiding.

The cultists are calling for there to be a limit on travel and they suggest using number plate reading cameras, facial recognition cameras and fuel rationing to control people. They say that medical diagnoses and treatments should be offered online and that all teaching should be done online (to reduce the amount of travel). They call anyone who questions their cult a 'domestic terrorist' or a 'climate denier'. The International Energy Agency has demanded that governments worldwide should introduce lockdown style restrictions to cut the use of oil and to ensure that global warming targets are met. (Despite this, the global warming cultists regularly feel the need to travel thousands of miles to attend conferences about climate change. Some of these conferences are attended by 20,000 delegates and, like most conventions and conferences, always seem to be held in interesting places where there are plenty of good hotels and which can be reached by good transportation.) A report submitted to the UK Government recommended that all airports except Heathrow, Glasgow and Belfast must close immediately and those three airports must close soon. The report says that the construction of new buildings must stop by 2050.

One group of lunatic greens claim that there will be 2,500 deaths a year in the UK from the heat by 2050. They obviously don't realise that 60,000 people a year die of the cold in the UK. If the temperature were to rise a little, those 60,000 lives might be saved. So, a higher temperature, if it were to happen, might kill 2,500 a year but would save 60,000 lives a year. Three cheers for global warming.

To maintain the myth that the world is getting hotter, news agencies simply claim that the weather is hotter than it really is. Today, for example, one major news agency reported that the temperature where I was had been 27.5 degrees C all day. However, a reliable thermometer reported a temperature of 15 degrees C (the same temperature as was reported by the Met office.)

The scientific nonsense shared with ignorant enthusiasm by global warming cultists sometimes beggars belief.

So, for example, in 'A Cry from the Far Middle', the American author P.J.O'Rourke pointed out that one adult's lungs will emit 2.3 pounds of carbon dioxide in a day. Given the size of the global population this means that human beings produce 17.25 trillion pounds of carbon dioxide every 24 hours. This, points out O'Rourke, is considerably higher than the 209 billion pounds of carbon dioxide produced by burning fossil fuels.

Things are made even worse when people take up strenuous exercise such as jogging or cycling. Exercise can multiply the carbon dioxide production by eight times.

It would be possible to argue that this may be why the conspirators behind the Great Reset are so keen to reduce the world's population to 500 million.

Finally, there are two primary sorts of individual who believe in global warming.

First, the conspirators who use global warming as a weapon.

Second, the unquestioning, witless and slightly insane enthusiasts who believe they have found a war to fight.

The BBC, which regards global warming as having been published in the Gospels, reports that a small army of volunteers is keeping so-called climate change deniers off Wikipedia. So much for freedom of speech and debate – yet again. These people are suppressing views they disagree with, and the BBC treats them as dedicated heroes. Wikipedia, which I regard as a fake encyclopaedia, is, I believe, the most dangerous site in the history of the internet.

But it is the silent collaborators, who say nothing and merely allow this dangerous myth to be promoted who are most dangerous.

There is not one jot of real scientific evidence for the myth of climate change. The myth was planned decades ago. Those who talk about flooding and disappearing cities are hysterical and deluded. Powerful, irresponsible media forces such as the BBC suppress debate about the climate in just the same way that they've suppressed debate about the rebranded flu. The hysteria is so acute that brain-dead protestors in the UK, protected by the police, happily stop ambulances.

People aren't threatened by climate change or the rebranded flu.

People are threatened by corruption too big for most people to see. They are threatened by self-serving, cowardly, virtue signalling, breast beating doctors, teachers and others whose wilful, staggering ignorance will result in hundreds of thousands of early and unnecessary deaths and massive, life-long ignorance.

It is important to remember that intellectually, spiritually, morally and politically there is absolutely no difference between the idiots who used to race around the countryside dressed in their second-best bed-sheets, with eye holes cut out in them, while carrying flaming crosses, and the idiots who glue themselves to roads and furniture or throw paint at innocent buildings. They are all deluded, misguided, barking and a threat to mankind and civilisation.

Government

There is some question about the nature of our governments. We are supposed to live in democracies but clearly this is not the case. Some say we live in a dictatorship. Others argue that we live in totalitarian states. A third suggestion is that our governments are communistic. Some of our leaders (those with a well-developed concept of the absurd) claim we live in a meritocracy. Here are some other possibilities:

Autocracy – rule by a government with absolute power
Chrysocracy – rule by the wealthy
Cosmocracy – rule by a world government
Cryptarchy – rule by a secret government
Diabolarchy – rule by devils
Kakistrocracy – rule by the worst citizens
Oligarchy – rule by the few
Plutocracy – rule by the wealthy
Technocracy – rule by people following rules written by technicians

Great Reset

The Great Reset is the end the conspirators are aiming for. They want to change society and introduce a comprehensive system of social credit.

Hate

In Canada, Trudeau is introducing an 'anti-hate' bill which will allow people to pre-emptively sue if they feel they are about to hear something hateful. Read that sentence again. This is what the woke and the politically correct lunatics have led us to. People in Canada will be able to sue if they think they may be about to be offended. How delighted the sanctimonious, humourless, censorious puritans must have been when they heard this.

Health Care

Once upon a time, many years ago, shortly after I had qualified as a doctor, I got a job as a GP. I'd always wanted to work as a GP and I'd worked in hospitals for just one year.

In those days, young doctors were thrown in at the deep end. When I sat down behind the desk to see my first patients, it was the first time I'd been in a doctor's surgery since I'd been poorly as a kid and my mum had taken me to see our GP. I can't remember what was wrong with me. I can however remember that the GP smoked a pipe and puffed at it constantly.

So, I sat down behind the desk and pressed a button which rang a bell in the waiting room. And then I started to look for the forms I'd need in order to write prescriptions, sick notes and so on. I didn't have a clue which forms were for what. I had to pop out and ask a receptionist to show me which forms to use for what.

Things were different in those days.

First, there was no appointments system.

Patients didn't ring up to fix an appointment a week, a fortnight or three weeks ahead. They just turned up in the morning or the evening. Five days a week. And Saturday mornings.

That was the first difference.

Second, there were no computers. Everything was far, far more efficient. Medical records were kept on bits of cardboard in a little folder. The folder went where the patient went.

The third difference was that if patients weren't well enough to make it to the surgery, or were too frail to manage a bus journey, they could ring up, or send a message if they didn't have a telephone and ask for the doctor to visit them at home. Lots of patients didn't have the telephone. I had some patients who didn't have electricity. You think I'm making this up but I'm not. I once took a consultant cardiologist to visit a patient of mine in his home. The cardiologist spent ages looking for a socket so that he could plug in his ECG machine. He was terribly disappointed when I told him there were no sockets because there was no electricity. They had oil lamps and a coal fire.

Sometimes if the patient were elderly or very ill or had just come out of hospital, the doctor would call in anyway – to see how things were. GPs even visited their patients when they were in hospital – just to check up on things. This wasn't special or unusual. This was normal.

And I'm not talking about 100 years ago. I'm talking about the 1970s.

Those of you who think I'm making this up, ask someone older. They'll confirm what I'm telling you. If you really want to know what it was like, I've written 15 books about a young country doctor in rural England.

I found that I learned more about people if I saw them in their own surroundings.

There was a fourth big difference.

Doctors didn't work the same sort of hours as accountants and librarians.

When I was a hospital doctor I worked ridiculous hours. When another junior doctor was on holiday, I worked a 168 hour week. Even when I was asleep I was on call and I didn't sleep more than two or three hours at a time.

And as a GP, I worked hours that would be considered ridiculous these days.

GPs used to provide a 24 hour service for 365 days a year. You could ring your GP any time of the day or night, weekends and bank holidays included. And he or she or a partner would come and visit. It would almost certainly be a doctor you knew or had seen before. At night I'd ask patients to turn on all the lights so that I could find their house quickly and easily. A doctor could take the patient's little cardboard records folder with him so that he was up-to-date and could add in anything new. Brilliantly simple. The record cards never seemed to get lost. And they never had an outage or a virus or got hacked.

And I have to say that night time visits were one of the best bits of being a GP. Driving home at 4.00 am, having helped someone out of a bad attack of asthma, it was impossible not to feel content. It was the only time of my life when I was up and around to see the sunrise.

And there was one other thing.

Doctors were very independent minded in those days. They didn't take kindly to being told what to do by bureaucrats and politicians.

But then things changed and everything went wrong.

It was the very beginning of the Great Reset – though I didn't realise it at the time; the start of the New World Order, the very beginning of the new normal.

The bureaucrats and the rule makers buggered up everything. They insisted that GPs introduced appointments systems and they created a health care system where patients are the least important element. At the time I thought it was merely a yearning to interfere for the sake of change. Now I know it was all deliberate. The conspirators wanted to bugger things up.

Britain, incidentally, was probably affected more than anywhere else in the world because Britain used to have the best GP service anywhere. Britain has gone from having the best family doctor service anywhere to having what is probably the worst. GPs still do night calls in other countries.

Today, the only place you're likely to come face to face with your GP is on the golf course.

In various books of mine I've written before about how things went wrong.

New rules about working hours and the end of a sense of vocation among young doctors all destroyed what we had. Doctors who retired were unable to keep their licences because of bureaucracy and something called 'revalidation'. The aim was to deprive communities of years' of wisdom and caring skills. It was all part of the plan to reduce the quality of health care and to kill people.

The service provided by GPs reached the pits in the early part of 2020 when many GPs pretty well closed their doors for no reasons other than misplaced fear, trust in drug company inspired government lies and, I'm afraid, good old-fashioned laziness.

If GPs had examined the evidence about the rebranded flu they would have seen through the tissue of lies deliberately and wickedly spread by politicians and advisors around the world. And, of course, they would have seen the truth about the experimental jabs which I have for many months now said will kill far, far more people than the rebranded flu.

Back in the mid-1970s, I wrote that doctors could no longer call themselves members of a profession since they took their orders from an industry – the drug industry. The medical establishment sold out decades ago and over the years I have been staggered by the way the BMA and the GMC have betrayed patients. Doctors have repeatedly allowed themselves to be tricked, cajoled and bought. Most now live in a cesspit of corruption where their professional lives are controlled by the most evil industry in the world.

Today, the medical profession is now totally controlled by the pharmaceutical industry – which is controlled by the conspirators.

Most cases of type II diabetes could be treated with diet rather than pills. Heart disease is treated with drugs or surgery when it has been proved beyond doubt that it can be treated successfully with diet, relaxation and exercise. Doctors have repeatedly misdiagnosed dementia. And they have prescribed huge quantities of dangerously addictive benzodiazepine drugs.

All that was bad enough.

But things got consistently worse during 2020 and 2021. Every day seemed to bring new examples of professional lunacy.

Unbelievably, and unforgivably, doctors writing in the British Medical Journal called for the medical profession to do less screening of patients and to cut back on prescribing treatment – 'to help combat climate change'. Doctors called for global warming concerns to be put above patients' interests.

Let's get this straight: the medical establishment wants to cut back on diagnosing cancer early in order to save Big Ben from disappearing under 100 foot waves a week on Wednesday. This is also terrifyingly wicked.

'The climate emergency is the true health crisis of our time,' is the message from the medical establishment. Doctors' leaders appear to have had their brains removed and replaced with those of 12-year-olds. The members of the medical establishment who believe this should all be certified insane and put into a coma to protect the public from their deranged utterings.

The nonsense from the BMA is pouring out these days.

For example, the BMA now says that Britain needs another 60,000 doctors.

Britain doesn't need any more doctors. Dare I suggest that the NHS needs the GPs on the payroll to do what they're paid for – which is to see patients. The Department of Health in the UK has reported that the average GP is now working a three day week and earning over £100,000.

Doctors protest that they are overworked and that they are struggling to deal with a continuing crisis. But they're working three day weeks! It's no wonder patients are more likely to win the lottery than get an appointment with their doctor.

Today, the medical profession is complicit in the Government's attack on the people it is paid to serve.

The Government repeatedly claims that Britain desperately needs more doctors.

But if the Government really wants to increase the number of GPs, it should invite retired GPs to emerge from retirement – and perhaps work part-time. (After all, many existing, younger GPs only work two or three days a week to reduce their tax liabilities. And that's part of the reason for the shortage. Older GPs working half a week each would improve the health service considerably.)

But this won't happen. The Government does not want older, experienced, independent-minded doctors working in Britain.

It is difficult to avoid the thought, by the way, that the GMC's absurd revalidation programme was deliberately introduced to force older, experienced, independent doctors out of the medical profession – thereby making it easier to destroy the NHS, to kill vast numbers of elderly and sick patients and to push through the rebranded flu hoax and the associated fraud involving an experimental injection.

Maybe the Government realised that older, more experienced doctors, not bound by an NHS contract, without mortgages to pay and without future careers to worry about, might be more likely to question the whole rebranded flu hoax. It is noteworthy that most of the few doctors objecting to the fraud have been older and more experienced physicians.

Having thousands of experienced doctors around would have made it difficult for the Government and the NHS to murder thousands of old people in care homes, nursing homes and hospitals. Most young doctors are, on the whole, far too naïve and self-serving to question authority. They don't understand the meaning of cognitive dissonance.

Here's more evidence proving that the genocide was real.

Private hospitals in the UK were paid billions of pounds to close their doors to private patients. The story was that they were being closed so that they could help support the overworked NHS during the pandemic. But the figures show that the NHS was never overworked. Indeed, parts of it – including intensive care wards – were quieter than usual. In order to ensure that the private health hospitals didn't interfere with the genocide, a total of 7,956 private beds were rented at £400 million a month. Taxpayers had a bill running into billions. But for 39% of the days paid for, those beds were completely empty. A total of 187 private hospitals were rented (together with their staff) but they treated an average of just eight covid patients a day. The vast majority of beds remained empty.

If private hospitals had remained open, umpteen thousands of patients would have been able to obtain treatment outside the NHS – or what is left of it. Patients with cancer and heart disease could have been treated.

And thousands of lives would have been saved.

But saving lives wasn't the Government's plan.

Today, in May 2022, as I write, there is, effectively, no GP service in the UK. Doctors insist on providing treatment by phone even though it has been proved beyond doubt to be unsafe. It is the total failure of the GP service which explains why the ambulance service cannot cope – and why people are waiting many hours for an ambulance needed urgently. It's why they stopped measuring waiting times in accident and emergency departments when they went over nine hours. It's why over 12 million people are or soon will be on urgent waiting lists and why they will probably never be scanned, X-rayed or treated. It's why death rates are soaring. None of this can possibly be through incompetence or accident.

Medical care is now far worse than it was in the 1950s. Deaths from untreated sepsis are soaring. Hospital staff insist that patients and visitors wear face coverings and practise social distancing, as though such actions will make any useful difference (in fact they are dangerous and will almost certainly cause much illness) but hospitals are dirtier than ever. I went into a hospital in Wales which was so disgusting that I wiped my feet when I left. The place was so filthy that no sensible farmer would store manure in it. Care assistants, with little or no training, have taken over work that nurses should be doing because the nurses are doing things that doctors should be doing. Tragically, nurses now seem to regard themselves as too important to do any caring. Time and time again I have seen reports in which patients and relatives have complained that nurses 'just didn't seem to care'. Charges will soon be introduced to see a GP because most family doctors made so much money out of jabbing that for tax reasons they're working three day weeks.

And don't think things are going to get any better.

Before the fake pandemic, UK ministers promised to speed up cancer diagnoses so that Britain would catch up with the rest of the world. But that's been abandoned. MPs have warned that just half of the patients with cancer are diagnosed at stage one or two. And, they say, things are going to get worse.

From March 2020 the service provided by most GPs (family doctors) in the UK has varied between appalling and virtually non-existent. Hospital care has been cut back because of pseudoscientific social distancing rules and pointless and damaging lockdowns but it is the GP service which has really been destroyed – by GPs themselves.

Could doctors really be so stupid as to believe the nonsensical statistics provided by the Government and its advisors? Were GPs cowed by the Government's threats that anyone who spoke out would lose their job and their licence to practise? If that were the case then those doctors should have been hounded out of their jobs and forced to retrain as traffic wardens. Or were many of those doctors simply lazy and eager to grab a chance to enjoy a long, well-paid holiday from their responsibilities?

During the cold winter months, patients who were allowed an appointment – usually with a nurse or assistant of some kind – were forced to wait outside in the rain and cold. Was this part of the culling process? Nothing would surprise me. Relatives were told that they could not accompany patients. This wasn't science or medicine. It was politicised black magic. Doctors complained that their 40 hour working week was too onerous. There was talk of GPs working one day a week because of the stress of the job. The establishment supported this.

It was by no means the first time that doctors have done crazy things because they were told to do them. Doctors deliberately removed yards of intestine because they were told it would help their patients. Other doctors removed or destroyed part of the human brain because they thought it would eradicate mental illness. Millions of patients became hooked on the hideously addictive benzodiazepine drugs because doctors were told they were safe and effective – and then ignored the evidence that they weren't and continued to prescribe them by the lorry load.

After March 2020, GPs in the UK started to demand that patients consult via the telephone or the internet. The evidence shows clearly that this is an impossible way to practise medicine. Diagnoses are missed and the death rate in the next year or two will rocket as a result. Patients are so disillusioned that they don't bother calling their GP – because they know that the service provided is darned near useless and virtually non-existent.

In the UK, there were between 25 and 27 million fewer appointments with GPs between March and August 2020 – 25 to 27 million fewer appointments than normal.

When the NHS bosses in the UK suggested that GPs should see more patients face to face, instead of insisting on treating patients on the phone or over the internet, the British Medical Association, the doctors' trade union (and in my view the patients' enemy) responded by complaining that the change was a reaction to media coverage 'rather than based on the needs of the profession'.

Does anyone in the BMA or the medical establishment give a damn about the needs of patients? I doubt it.

And yet, miraculously, GPs in the UK managed to see their

patients when they were giving thousands of covid 19 jabs – at £12 something per jab. Indeed, the rush to push needles into innocent and ignorant members of the public has been another excuse for the fact that GPs cannot provide a half-way decent service for their patients.

The basic problem is that today's medical schools (like all schools and university departments) deliberate teach half-truths; they never teach students how to think or criticise the system. After all, what system is going to teach people to question itself?

Students are educated by rote; taught in the way that dogs are taught tricks. Wisdom is a disadvantage. Common sense is eradicated. Young doctors are incapable of making informed decisions and that suits the pharmaceutical industry just fine. If you don't question perceived notions then how do you ever learn?

Young doctors are never exposed to the truth or to the questioning of 'accepted' beliefs or to proper debate with those who question the way things are done. Because of my habit of questioning authority I used to be invited to speak at medical and nursing schools. That is no longer allowed, and so medical schools churn out platoons of unquestioning prescription signing zombies.

Good doctors need insight, imagination and intuition and the capacity to make diagnostic leaps; sideways if necessary. Good doctors need to be able to observe and they need to be able to think. Great discoveries are invariably made by outsiders and mavericks. Today, such skills are not simply encouraged; they are now not allowed. As a result, the medical profession is packed with drudges, unthinking, too frightened of losing their jobs to show any spirit.

NHS doctors are employed by the Government; they are civil servants and they are bought: body, mind and soul. They do not seem to have the courage to stand up for whatever principles they might have. They do not dare disagree with their administrative bosses because they are hired hands. They do not dare stick up for their patients because they live in fear of bureaucratic censure. And so they vaccinate, and they perform unnecessary operations and they prescribe drugs which they should know are unsafe. Tonsils and lengths of intestine are ripped out by surgeons who don't seem to have the foggiest notion of the harm they are doing. Healthy breasts are slashed off unnecessarily.

Doctors do not have the courage to stand up for their patients because they have lost their independence; they are simply civil servants; they have sold their souls for a fat salary, short working hours and a wonderful pension. They are so beholden to their employers that they dare not even stand up to bullying, they dare not even speak out when they see things happening which they know, in their hearts, are wrong. Their spirits have curdled.

The modern medical establishment elevates its official beliefs into an orthodoxy, always suggesting that they are right because they are, well, right and that the absence of evidence is not to be allowed to interfere with the acceptance of their conclusions. This is tabloid science.

For example, the supporters of vaccination deal with their opponents not by debate but by denouncing anyone who disagrees. It's the same approach as is used by global warming advocates. Critics armed with science are demonised in the same way as critics of the climate change nonsense are demonised and dismissed as flat-earthers or global warming deniers.

Anyone who disagrees with the establishment is a dangerous heretic – to be excluded from all debates, and condemned and isolated.

Science in general and the medical profession in particular have been hijacked by politically correct lobbyists. Dissenters, daring to question the new orthodoxy of the group-think obsessionals, are guilty of thought crime and to be vilified and suppressed. Group think unoriginality oppresses and suppresses.

Any doctor who does not stick to the rules will be refused a licence and prevented from practising. Any doctor who questions or in any way criticises the official view of vaccination will be removed from the medical register before you can say 'scientific bigotry'.

It is today more dangerous for a doctor to be ahead of his time (which is to say, critical of well-established but ill-advised and dangerously nonsensical medical practices) than it is for him to be behind his time. The doctor who dares to criticise the acknowledged mainstream is a dangerous heretic who must be crushed.

Over the last five decades I have made many forecasts about medical hazards. Most have already been proved entirely accurate. But accuracy is no defence against ridicule, abuse, scorn and scepticism; indeed, since being correct makes the authoritarians fearful, the ridicule, abuse, scorn and scepticism are enhanced. No part of the mainstream media, or the important internet platforms, allows me to share provable truths.

They have been preparing for the Great Reset for many years.

The common purpose controlled medical establishment has for years now been suppressing dissent and debate – especially on issues which might prove essential for the development of the New World Order.

And so doctors have stayed silent when they should have spoken out.

Many doctors of my age and experience are ashamed of the medical profession they see now.

Is it going to change? Are things going to improve?

I fear not.

Doctors are too happy with the present state of affairs. They're doing very little work and making tons of money.

And now doctors want to work entirely at home – using the internet for everything they do and relying on computers and robots.

Doctors seem unconcerned about the fact that there is solid, reliable evidence proving that doctors who try to make diagnoses over the telephone, or with the aid of a camera and a computer, make far more mistakes than doctors who take the trouble to see their patients either in their consulting rooms, in hospitals or in their homes. Today, I read about a woman who had been diagnosed by video link and told that she had terminal liver failure. A face to face examination was refused. Eventually, the woman went to an A&E department and was diagnosed with an infection treatable with antibiotics.

The irony is that computers and robots are more efficient and safer than doctors working through cameras and telephones.

The only advantage doctors have over technology is the placebo healing response that comes from a doctor seeing and talking to a patient. The placebo response can give a massive uplift to the efficacy of a treatment.

But doctors are denying their patients that advantage.

Doctors are betraying their patients and the once respectable profession of medicine.

Future health care will be managed entirely through the internet.

Anyone planning to study medicine should abandon their hopes. There is no future for medical practice.

In future, medicine will be closely linked to social credit.

Only those with suitably high social credit scores will be entitled to any medical treatment.

Houses

In the world of the Great Reset, ordinary people will not be allowed to own their own homes. The widely promoted principle 'you will own nothing and you will be happy' will apply to buying and owning any sort of property as much as it will apply to anything else.

Prices of homes all around the world have been pushed very high as big investment companies have moved in and bought thousands of homes at a time – helping to push up prices and force out private buyers. At the same time, the quality of housing has fallen dramatically. Builders who obey EU laws about house construction invariably produce shoddy, poorly built properties which are not designed to last.

It is worth noting that houses in Japan are built to last 30 years. After that they either fall down or they are knocked down and replaced.

The process of destroying the long established principle of home ownership is already well under way. Interest rates are rising (and likely to continue to rise for years, as central banks appear to struggle to control the runaway inflation they created). Rising interest rates will make it more difficult for new buyers to get their feet onto the bottom of the property ladder and they will make it increasingly difficult for those who own homes to hang onto them. Constantly rising energy prices will add to the expense of owning a home – particularly if the home is old and poorly insulated. Banning Russians from property ownership will also reduce prices.

Worse still, the Government in the UK is forcing 15 million house owners to make such massive and ruinously expensive changes to their homes that the only practical solution will be to knock down perfectly good, solid homes.

The energy performance certificates which must now be linked to every home are to be revised in 2025 to include a variety of untested, unpopular, expensive inefficient eco-inventions which are popular with the conspirators (and the global warming cultists who represent their views in the media and the political market place).

So, houses which have remote controlled thermostats will have a better rated energy performance. And so will houses which are fitted with heat pumps – the absurdly expensive to fit and expensive to run replacements for traditional gas boilers. Heat pumps cost up to £22,000 to have fitted and cost four times as much to run as gas boilers. Heat pumps also require electricity, and since most electricity will for many years be obtained from fossil fuels and from burning wood pellets (imported into the UK from across the Atlantic) the logic is difficult to understand.

The absence of logic hasn't stopped politicians embracing heat pumps (and many other absurd eco inventions) and those who choose to prefer more traditional, more sensible forms of heating a home will be punished.

Landords who rent out homes have already been told that after 2027 it will be illegal to lease properties which are not highly rated.

Within a few years, homes which do not satisfy the new requirements will be unsaleable. Home owners who don't have a heat pump fitted will not be allowed to sell their home. Sadly, however, the cost of running a home fitted with a heat pump will mean that home owners who do have a heat pump fitted will not be able to sell their home because it will be considered too expensive to run.

And, of course, the conspirators want us all living in high rise apartment blocks. There will be no pets and the apartments will be small and identical. Everything will be controlled centrally. And if the conspirators want to control the people living in an apartment building, they can do so easily by locking the entrance doors. This, of course, is what was happening in China in April and May 2022 when the authorities decided to pursue their absurd zero covid policy. Apartment buildings were firmly shut and the inhabitants were refused permission to leave.

Home prices will fall notably over the next decade or so. The homeless will be forced into new, tiny, cardboard flats in approved city centres but if your social credit rating is poor you will find it difficult or impossible to rent a home of your own.

So what does the future hold for those with poor social credit ratings?

Well, of course, one of the principle tenets of the Great Reset is that the global population will be reduced to 500 million.

But until then where will all the homeless live?

Maybe in something similar to the debtors' prisons which Dickens portrayed so well. Alternatively, the streets will be full of penniless, vagrant families wrapped in any clothes they possess. In cold weather they will keep warm with layers of cardboard and, if they are lucky, a tattered, dirty old sleeping bag or two.

How they Plan to Bankrupt us all

It all begins, of course, with the Global Reset, which doesn't include any provision for private property – unless you're already a billionaire or a member of the British royal family. They don't want us to own anything because people who own a home or a pension or who have a few quid in the bank have an unacceptable tendency to assume that they are free citizens. They want to remove every last vestige of our independence and they'll be ruthless.

(If you don't believe me check out the Agenda 21 promotional guff, as published by the United Nations. And take a look at Pope Francis's words on private property.)

So, how are they planning to take away our private property?

Silly question, I'm afraid, because they've already started their five point plan to bankrupt us all.

First, of course, crashing the global economy has damaged the value of any investments you may have. Unless you work for the State and have one of their protected pensions your retirement fund will have been savagely damaged. Wrecking the economy was deliberate; it is part of the Agenda 21 plan. Billionaires such as Gates and Musk did amazingly well during 2020 – their wealth grew massively. Remember the Rothschilds at the end of the Battle of Waterloo? They tricked all the other traders into thinking that Napoleon had won and then cleaned up and made a huge fortune.

Second, they have reduced interest rates to a level never seen before. If you have a million pounds sitting in your Government savings account, the annual interest will just about buy you a tankful of petrol. (As long as you only have a small car).

Third, the crashing economy will destroy millions of jobs. The United Nations said in 2020 that 50% of all jobs are going to disappear, and we can trust them because it's their game, their ball and their packet of sandwiches. Those without jobs will have to rely on government handouts – renamed the universal basic income.

Fourth, if you own your own home, or think you do, or you own part of it, then you're in trouble. Interest rates are going to remain the lowest in history for a while – to make sure that those with savings see their savings slowly disappear. And then interest rates will go up. Not a bit. But a lot. And when interest rates are up to 8, 9 or 10 per cent – or even higher – imagine what mortgage payments will reach. They'll be even higher. And most people won't be able to afford to keep their homes. That will be end of private home ownership and another step towards the Great Reset.

Fifth, why are interest rates going to soar? Well, because inflation is high and interest rates will rise to try to bring inflation down. (Remember too, that high rates of inflation also destroy any savings that people have hung onto.)

Oh, and there is a sixth trick up their sleeve: taxes.

Governments everywhere have been throwing money around with great joy. Ten billion here, a hundred billion there. They'll need to replenish the coffers and pay off the debts. And so taxes are going to rise. They'll invent new taxes you've never dreamt of – and the main aim will not just be to raise money but to impoverish everyone.

They don't want us to own anything. It's the plan.

And when we're all impoverished, they will generously pay us all a universal basic income and we will then be entirely dependent on Bill Gates, Klaus Schwab and co for our daily bread. If we misbehave or criticise our masters then our payment won't come through and our digital bank account will remain empty. That's where the social credit system comes in.

Remember: the people controlling the system are not inept or incompetent. They are deceitful, devious and far more wicked than anything most of us have ever come across.

When I was a GP, I worked as a police surgeon for some years. I have met, examined and interviewed a number of murderers. I never met any as evil as the deceitful and devious politicians, scientists and doctors now determined to destroy everything we value – for power and money. Make no mistake about it, the end of civilisation is coming towards us at the speed of light.

Inflation

In July 2021, I put a note on my websites saying this: 'I've been warning for many months of a massive rise in inflation and it is coming. Printing money was bound to create massive national debts. An unofficial currency devaluation is inevitable. Bankruptcies are going to increase massively.'

It was many months before the Bank of England admitted that their 2% inflation target had been well and truly breached – and that inflation was going to get much, much worse. They pretended it was all out of their hands, and a complete surprise.

Inflation will be welcomed by politicians because it will further damage individuals and small businesses, boost the power of the State and lead us speedily into the Great Reset and the social credit system which the conspirators have been dreaming about for years.

There is a wide misunderstanding about inflation but it has always had a devastating impact on our lives.

In 1931 you could rent a house in the English countryside which had 5 reception rooms, 17 bedrooms, 6 bathrooms, a garage and four cottages, gardens, a lake stocked with trout and 1,650 acres. You could rent all that for £375 a year.

Inflation in the UK in the 1970s hit 27% and it was a steal if you could borrow money at 15%. How many people could pay mortgages at 20% today?

Central banks (such as the Bank of England) have kept interest rates at all-time lows. In many countries (such as Japan), interest rates have been held in negative territory for some years – with lenders paying banks money to allow them to store their savings with them.

But in the early spring of 2022 it eventually became obvious even to the central bankers that they had to confess that inflation was rising fast and out of control.

(We should remember, by the way, that the official inflation figures are something of a joke since everyone knows that the real inflation figure was already more than 20% in early 2022. The official inflation figures don't cover essential bills. Many important bills are doubling or more but will not be covered in the official inflation figures.)

Either central bankers (such as the wildly overpaid employees at the Bank of England) failed to see that inflation was going to soar or failed to do something about it (in either case they were woefully, egregiously, incompetent) or they deliberately allowed inflation to soar out of control in order to help destroy their economies to help prepare the way for the Great Reset.

The last inflation spike occurred in 1992 when it hit 8%.

There is, however, one big difference this time.

In 1992, interest rates were at 12%. (Borrowing rates were much higher than that, of course.) With inflation at 8% this meant that for the banks the real cost of borrowing money was 4%. In the 1970s, inflation hit 20% in the UK and interest rates were 16% so, again, the real cost of borrowing money was 4%.

Today, the figures are very different.

Inflation is officially around 8% but interest rates are 1%. This means that those borrowing money are still getting a bargain. The money they borrow is being devalued at a much faster rate than their cost of borrowing it. The result is that debts are being erased very quickly. There is a great incentive for people and companies to borrow as much as they can. Since millions of individuals and many companies already have far too much debt, this is clearly a route to disaster. Companies which have no future will be kept alive because they can borrow as much as they like at a rate of -7% or more. The higher inflation goes the bigger the problem will become unless interest rates are raised higher than inflation rates. This won't happen, of course, for two reasons. First, governments want inflation to get rid of the debts they recklessly accumulated in the last few years. Second, millions of home owners would no longer be able to pay their mortgages and the housing market would collapse. The Bank of England is pretending that it is dealing with inflation by pushing up interest rates by a quarter of a point at a time. These tiny rises in the cost of borrowing money won't make any difference at all.

Things are equally bizarre in the Eurozone where the deposit rate has been minus 0.5% since 2014 (in other words people lending money to the European Central Bank had to pay money to the bank for the privilege) and the inflation rate is now 7.4% (at least). This means that the real cost of borrowing money is around 8% (and savers are losing 8% on their savings every year.)

There is another reason for keeping interest rates absurdly low even though inflation is soaring ahead: the cautious and thrifty are seeing their hard earned savings destroyed by savings. If you have saved £1,000 towards your retirement, the combination of high inflation and low interest rates mean that the spending power of your £1,000 is diminishing (officially) by £80 or so a year. In reality, because inflation is much higher than the official figure, the spending power of your £1,000 is falling by £200 a year. In just a few years' time that £1,000 of savings will be worthless.

All this fits neatly into the Great Reset and the new social credit paradigm.

Remember those infamous words: 'You will own nothing and be happy'.

Most people have never seen inflation in action and they don't regard it as a big threat. They'd probably put it somewhere between a slipping roof tile and a parking ticket. They probably haven't heard of Germany in the 1920s when workmen received half their pay at midday and the rest before they went home because of inflation. Housewives put their currency notes into a wheelbarrow when they went to the shops. And most people's life savings weren't enough to buy a single postage stamp.

If you trust the central banks, and the Bank for International Settlements, then you needn't worry too much about inflation.

But if you don't believe that the central banks (and the BIS) have your best interests at heart then you should be worried.

No, forget that.

You should be terrified.

By destroying savings and impoverishing us all, inflation will help usher in the Great Reset and the world of social credit.

Law

The main purpose of the law is to protect life and property.

Under the Great Reset, we will own nothing (not even our own bodies, which already belong to the State and which can be used for transplants when we die) and so, in theory at least, there will be little or no requirement for any laws. The conspirators will own everything and regardless of whether this results in collectivism or crony capitalism the result will be communism.

The conspirators want to remove our humanity, our kindness, our independence, our conscious, our dignity and our decency because these are concepts they don't understand and which they regard as irrelevant and unnecessary.

There are more laws in the developed world than at any other time in history. And yet, paradoxically, there is more lawlessness. Some of it cruel and some of it is petty. Much of it illustrates the sense of a lack of respect for others which has been encouraged for decades and which has been augmented by a sense of greed and a great sense of entitlement.

When my friend's relative collapsed and died in the street (in daylight) the first person on the scene stole his wallet and his smart, brogue shoes and hurried away to leave someone else to ring for an ambulance.

When a friend's mother died, the nursing home staff removed all her rings. At the mortuary my friend's father noticed that the rings were missing. A few days later my friend asked the nursing home staff what had happened to the jewellery.

'Oh, we put them in an envelope to keep for you,' he was told by a red-faced 'nurse', producing a brown envelope from a drawer in the office desk.

I have heard other people report the same deceit and I have absolutely no doubt that if the rings had not been missed, and my friend had not enquired about them, they would have been sold and the proceeds shared out among the staff.

Leisure

There are clear signs that the conspirators orchestrating the Great Reset are determined to delete all signs of history from our civilisation. The removal of statues and memorials (usually because of some rather flimsy connections with slavery) is just a superficial example of what is clearly a determined plan to eradicate all signs of our culture.

And the conspirators are leaving no small aspects of our culture untouched.

So, for example, curious things have been happening in television, film and theatre. The title role in 'Dr Who' (a role traditionally played by a man) was given to a woman and then to a black actor. The iconic 007 identification number for James Bond (a quintessentially white male) was given to a black woman. At least one black woman has played Hamlet.

On several occasions, producers took up options on books of mine about a young doctor working in the English countryside in the 1970s. But each time the producers confessed that they couldn't get financing unless they made the doctor black or Asian or something other than white. The same thing happened with a novel about a young man who inherited a golf course – also in the same period. They agreed that the change would have altered the nature of the story, but unless the character's skin colour was changed no financiers would produce any money. The irony is that if I had written a book about a black or Asian character I would have been accused of cultural appropriation.

I know that those involved will say that I'm wrong, biased and stuck in a time warp, but it sometimes seems to me that these things are done to make a point – though the only point I can see is that all sacred shibboleths must be sacrificed on the altar of the Great Reset.

I have heard it said, no doubt in jest, that to win prizes in theatre, film and literature it is preferable to be black or female or describable as 'ethnic' in some way, and preferably all three. I have heard it said, also presumably in jest, that to be a one parent mother and a recovering drug addict might be considered a bonus. Jests are dangerous these days; anyone who said such a thing in public would be pilloried and then ruined.

Life Expectation

In April and May 2020 I warned that deaths from the lockdowns, and resulting closure of health care services, would far exceed the number of deaths from the rebranded flu. (I warned about the lockdowns in my book 'Coming Apocalypse' which was published in April 2020.)

And it quickly became clear that this warning was entirely justified.

Now there is evidence showing that the average Briton can expect to live nine months less because of the absurd and unnecessary closure of services by GPs and hospitals.

Delayed diagnoses and delayed treatment for cancer and heart disease are the cause of the fall in life expectancy.

Financial analysts report that pension providers are expected to gain £7.4 billion in profits over the next five years – as a direct result of the lower life expectancy.

A fall in life expectancy will, of course, fit in perfectly with the aims of those promoting the Great Reset.

Meanwhile, the evidence shows that those countries which did not put their citizens under house arrest, have suffered far fewer deaths than those countries which did.

The long-term effect of the most egregiously stupid public policies in history, and the failure of public health management, will be to take many nations back into the Dark Ages.

The British 'Partygate' scandal, which revealed that senior politicians and civil servants were regularly partying in private while publicly forbidding relatives from visiting the sick and the dying, banning weddings and keeping loved ones apart, seemed to me to prove that the politicians, advisors and others knew that the lockdowns had nothing to do with medicine but were simply part of a long-running programme designed to create fear and promote compliance.

As a result of the Partygate scandal, the UK's Prime Minister, Boris Johnson and scores of politicians and civil servants were fined a modest £50 each for breaking the lockdown rules that they themselves had created. The police were accused of failing to investigate fully and it appears that no one was fired. Neither the Prime Minister nor the Chancellor of the Exchequer (both of whom had lied and been fined) resigned.

Members of the British public were not dealt with quite so leniently. Among the other 136,000 people fined for breaking the lockdown rules were the following: a student was fined £10,000 for organising a snowball fight; a pub landlord who held a Christmas gathering the same night that Downing Street had a party was fined £4,000 and, almost unbelievably, a beggar was fined £434 for holding out his cap at King's Cross station in London. What sort of police officer would report a beggar? What sort of magistrate would impose such a fine?

Long Covid

In the spring of 2022, the UK Government said that there were officially nearly two million people in Britain suffering from 'long covid' – and that the figure was rising fast.

A report from the US suggested that around 12 million Americans were alleged to have long covid.

Politicians, medical advisors and journalists claimed that up to 12% of all those who'd had covid still had symptoms 12 weeks later – and nearly half of all long covid sufferers had symptoms a year later. Long covid was blamed as the biggest single reason for inefficiency, falling production levels and staff shortages. It is also said to be a big reason for the collapsing global economy and for soaring inflation.

That's what Governments claim, and it's rather odd because the biggest and most significant research into long covid, conducted in France, concluded that long covid is about as real as mare's nests and the Loch Ness Monster. It is largely a psychological problem rather than a real physical disease.

The fact checkers disapproved of the research, of course, but they live in cloud cuckoo land where the rebranded flu is a deadly plague, covid jabs are safe and effective and every Christmas Eve, Klaus Schwab straps on a white beard, becomes Father Christmas and squeezes down every chimney in the land.

So, if long covid doesn't exist what is going on?

Why do millions of people claim to be suffering from it and why do governments agree with their self-diagnoses? It is acknowledged that many of the long covid 'sufferers' will never go back to work.

Government statistics prove that there was never a pandemic but now we have a global long covid pandemic.

Before going on, it is important to understand that it has been recognised for decades that the ordinary flu can occasionally leave patients feeling physically weak and depressed. Post viral fatigue syndrome (long flu, if you like) is real but it is relatively uncommon and, compared to long covid, it tends to be short lived.

So, why have they created this fake disease?

First, we have to remember that governments handed out huge sums of money to allow millions to stay at home for 2020 and 2021. If you have been paid to stay at home and do nothing for a year it is difficult to get out of the habit of getting up at 10.00 am and spending the day watching TV or playing computer games.

None of this was accidental, of course.

The absurd schemes whereby governments gave healthy people huge sums of money to do nothing were deliberately designed to help wreck the global economy. Governments have deliberately created an army of malingerers who have got used to the idea of being paid to do absolutely nothing. It's the beginning of the universal basic income – a critical part of the Great Reset.

Long covid was tailor made for malingerers who also happen to have been turned into hypochondriacs.

Second, governments welcomed the growth in the number of alleged covid sufferers because it helps make people afraid of the rebranded flu – and accept the jabs which were dishonestly promoted as preventing it.

Third, governments know that if a huge chunk of the workforce stays at home, the disruption and the cost will severely damage the economy. And that, of course, is part of the conspirators' plan. Destroying the global economy is the reason for the absurd, destructive and unsustainable net zero project – abandoning fossil fuels and replacing oil, gas and coal with inefficient solar power, wind power and, most absurd of all, biomass. (It's also the reason for the manufactured wars which are going to be a permanent part of our lives.)

Fourth, and this is crucial, the false long covid disease is an excellent cover for the injuries caused by the jabs given to protect against the rebranded flu. Remember, long covid only appeared after people in trials were given the jabs.

And just look at the problems known to be caused by the jabs and by long covid.

Here are ten of the commonest side effects associated with the widely promoted experimental jabs. These just happen to be ten of the commonest symptoms associated with long covid: heart problems, stroke, clotting disorders, joint pains, convulsions and other neurological problems, Bell's palsy, Guillain Barre syndrome, autoimmune disease, respiratory problems, mental health troubles and fatigue. What a coincidence: the problems caused by long covid are exactly the same as the problems caused by the jabs!

Naturally, the mainstream media won't discuss or debate any of this. Governments, advisors, journalists and the medical profession all follow the same line – they are all conspirators and all part of the conspiracy. Anyone who dares to look at the evidence – and expose the truth – is dismissed as a conspiracy theorist and banned from sharing their views.

Looking

Life is now difficult for exhibitionists of all kinds – whether they are celebrities promoting films, records, shows, autobiographies or simply themselves, or cultists promoting an unscientific obsession with some curious belief (such as the thought that the world is getting so hot that we will all soon boil to death, like hapless lobsters).

The celebrity exhibitionists pay fortunes to dress themselves in ever-more outlandish, provocative outfits in the hope that people, especially those armed with cameras, will look at them and admire their appearance.

The cultist exhibitionists glue themselves to the road, hold up ambulances and throw paint at buildings in the hope that people, especially those carrying cameras, will look at them and admire their steadfast dedication to a myth.

They are now all wasting their time. At least, if they are in England they are wasting their time.

A new law has made staring illegal. It's a serious law. A man in England was sent to prison for staring at a woman. There will doubtless be many more cases. But when does looking become staring? And when does open-eyed day-dreaming become staring for that matter? Is it acceptable to look at a bus? Or will the passengers on the bus all claim that you are staring at them? Is it acceptable to watch people playing football in a park? Is it a criminal offence to look at a bride coming out of a church on the arm of her new husband?

What do you do on a crowded train? Looking into the distance, as though concentrating on something 1000 miles away is dangerous. Someone at the far end of the carriage could easily assume that you were looking at them. Modern egos are large and well decorated with a potent mixture of vanity, paranoia and an awareness of the ego owner's rights.

The only safe thing to do is to do what everyone else is doing: look at the screen of your smart phone where you can stare at the celebrities and the exhibitionists quite safely.

Mainstream Journalism

A mainstream journalist (whether working in print or broadcast journalism) is someone who tells lies for money. This is nothing new, of course. The Guardian and the Daily Mail are propaganda sheets which employ would-be journalists who can't get proper jobs. The BBC is a narrowcaster which concentrates on fake news and misinformation.

Journalists have always lied and exaggerated and done the bidding of corrupt proprietors and demanding advertisers.

The odd thing is that tabloid newspapers have always been more reputable than the broadsheets. The tabloids know that people are watching them but the broadsheet journalists think they can get away with massive deceits. Television programmes are even more disreputable than the broadsheets and television journalists, though nauseatingly sanctimonious, are far more dishonest than any other class of journalists. The BBC is, of course, a good example of this.

Sadly, things have got far, far worse since the early spring of 2020.

The whole of the mainstream media has been bought with millions of dollars and pounds of taxpayers' money. Years ago the organs of the mainstream media sacked the experienced journalists and brought in hundreds of left wing, millennial snowflakes who were so stupid, greedy and bigoted that they were easy to corrupt. The BBC recruited a gazillion really stupid Guardian reading communists to replace the proper journalists who were once employed there. No one at the BBC, ITV, Sky or any other mainstream channel TV or radio channel will dare to broadcast the truth. I've been challenging them for two years. Silence. They're prejudiced and bent. No honesty and no guts. They steadfastly refuse to debate vaccination, climate change or any of the big issues. Why? If they believed what they say, surely they'd be eager to prove that they were right in a national, live, network debate.

Media doctors around the world have been making big money promoting the official menu of lies. Anyone with a PhD in anything calls themselves doctor and makes big money.

Journalists used to challenge authority. Now they delight in cheering, supporting and promoting the conspirators. They accept honours and invitations to dine and party with the people they should be holding to account.

Sadly, mainstream journalists and broadcasters have sold their integrity.

It sometimes seems to me that they enjoy attacking and smearing the honest truth-telling doctors and scientists. Maybe it is their way of dealing with the guilt they must feel.

Maskitis

The UK Government has admitted that there is no evidence that face coverings stop any bugs spreading. Anyone who has ever worn a face covering because they thought it would keep them safe from covid was misled, lied to, falsely reassured and, to be blunt, behaving irrationally. Many people in power continue to insist that people wear them, and they do this to remind people that nothing is normal –nor ever will be. The greens don't seem to care that more plastic is used to make the billions of face coverings which are used than was employed in making the plastic bags they hated so much. They don't care about the birds and other wildlife being harmed by discarded face coverings.

We have entered the Great Reset and face coverings are there to remind us of our slavery.

Anyone who wears a face covering today is suffering from a new disease which I have identified as chronic maskitis.

Chronic maskitis sufferers will have almost certainly believed everything they've been told by their government, by the media and by the small army of media doctors now forever repeating the officially inspired lies.

Way back in the early summer of 2020, I published material proving that face coverings were useless and certain to do more harm than good. At that time, Fauci and Whitty agreed that wearing a face covering was a pointless and dangerous thing to do. Fauci referred to the wearing of face coverings as virtue signalling.

In March 2020, Dr Jenny Harries, Deputy Chief Medical Officer in the UK, warned that it is possible to trap the virus in a face covering and start breathing it in. She said that wearing a face covering was not a good idea. Professor Chris Whitty, the UK's Chief Medical Officer, said that wearing a face covering had almost no effect on reducing the risk of contracting covid-19, and that the Government did not advise healthy individuals to wear face coverings.

But then, for no good reason that I could see, the official line changed – virtually overnight. People were told that they should wear face coverings. Children in school were forced to wear face coverings all day long. Medical staff and some shop assistants wore them with their visors, their goggles, their plastic gowns and their rubber gloves.

In June 2021, I was becoming so worried by the madness that I made a video arguing that most wearers of face coverings would be dead or demented in ten years.

Not surprisingly, vital evidence outlining the dangers and ineffectiveness of wearing face coverings has been banned, hidden or deleted from the internet. Public discussion and debate about the value of face masks has for 18 months now been suppressed by politicians and the media. The people at Google and YouTube will be directly responsible for millions of deaths. So will media doctors, people with PhDs and crooked fact-checkers who've supported their government's lies.

In 2020, I wrote a book explaining how and why face coverings do more harm than good. The book contains scientific references explaining precisely why face coverings are dangerous and don't do what people are told they will do. The book, which listed scores of relevant scientific papers, was banned, of course.

It's worth remembering that thousands of years ago, it was discovered that forcing people to wear coverings over their faces broke their will and made them subservient. Face coverings depersonalise the wearers and dehumanised them. More recently, CIA torture techniques include forcing people to wear face coverings.

The big problem with face coverings is that the reduced oxygen intake is accompanied by an increase in carbon dioxide intake. The tighter a face covering fits the more likely it is to reduce blood oxygen levels and to increase the amount of carbon dioxide being inhaled. This is a real hazard. And then there is the problem that lower oxygen levels and increased levels of carbon dioxide stimulate greater inspiratory flow – leading to a greater risk that loose fibres from the face covering will be inhaled. Studies have shown that loose fibres are seen on all types of face coverings and may be inhaled causing serious lung damage. One risk is pulmonary fibrosis – a disease which cannot be cured and has a poor survival rate.

Then there is the fact that face coverings simply don't work. Between 2004 and 2016, at least twelve articles appeared in medical and scientific journals showing that face coverings do not prevent the transmission of infection. And those tests were with approved face coverings rather than face coverings made out of old dish cloths, bras and bits of unwanted dress material. Cloth face coverings fail to impede or stop flu virus transmissions, and the number of layers of fabric required to prevent pathogen penetration would require a suffocating number of layers and could not be used.

The World Health Organisation, which originally opposed face masks, now recommends that disposable masks should be worn and discarded after one use. And the evidence shows that they should be changed every two hours. Few people can afford to buy six masks a day and so masks are frequently worn more than once. This massively increases the risk of a chest infection developing. Bacterial pneumonia is a real risk among those wearing face coverings.

There are lots of specific risks.

Way back in September 2020, a group of 70 doctors pointed out that children are badly affected by having to wear face masks. 'Mandatory face masks in schools are a major threat to their development,' they wrote. Dentists in New York reported seeing a number of patients with inflamed gums and other problems due to masks. It is likely that anyone who wears a face covering for long periods will have a damaged immune system – and be more susceptible to infection. Studies have shown that hypoxia can inhibit immune cells used to fight viral infections. Low oxygen levels reduce T cells and therefore reduce immunity levels.

Moreover, while the wearer of a face covering thinks that they are becoming accustomed to re-breathing exhaled air, the problems within the brain are growing as the oxygen deprivation continues. Brain cells which die, because of a shortage of oxygen, will never be replaced. They are gone forever. A leading neurologist has pointed out that children and teenagers must never wear masks, partly because they have extremely active and adaptive immune systems but also because their brains are especially active and vulnerable. The more active an organ is the more oxygen it needs. And so the damage to children's brains is huge and irreversible. She warns that dementia is going to increase in ten years, and the younger generation will not be able to reach their potential because they have been wearing face coverings.

Chronic maskitis sufferers are likely to suffer skin problems too. A dermatologist has warned that face coverings trap warm moisture that is produced when we exhale. For those with acne, this can lead to acne flares. For many others, this warm, moist environment creates the perfect condition for naturally occurring yeast and bacteria to flourish and grow more abundant. This overgrowth of yeast and bacteria can produce angular cheilitis, the cracking and sores at the corners of the mouth.

And face coverings cause eye problems too. Eye specialists say that chronic maskitis sufferers should wear goggles all day. Not dark glasses. Goggles. Swimming goggles, skiing goggles.

And there is another big worry.

Cancer patients who are in remission are more likely to find their cancer coming back if they wear a face covering – because of the low oxygen levels.

The truth is that wearing a face covering was introduced as part of the programme of fear designed to force people to become compliant – so that they would accept whatever else they were ordered to do.

And the authorities know that those who wear masks will die sooner than those who don't.

Medicine Shortages

It isn't just food that is going to be in short supply as the conspirators push us further and further into the Great Reset in preparation for a world ruled by social credit.

Medicine shortages have also arrived in the UK and almost certainly the rest of Europe.

Menopausal women have noticed a dramatic shortage of HRT and hay-fever sufferers may have to hunt around to find anti-histamines they need to quell their seasonal symptoms.

I have no doubt that Brexit will be blamed for the shortages but that is the slick, quick, politically correct answer.

The truth is that the delays, fuel shortages and other problems caused by the deadly sanctions against Russia are also responsible for exacerbating the shortages of essential drugs which may soon overwhelm us and add to our misery.

Is it all accidental and unforeseeable?

Of course not.

The conspirators don't do accidental and they don't do unforeseeable.

The medicine shortages are all part of the Great Reset.

Essential, life-saving drugs (such as those used to treat cancer, heart disease and type 1 diabetes) could soon be as difficult to find as mare's nests and hen's teeth.

Whenever you possibly can, my advice is to stock up on essential medicines – especially ones you can buy over the counter without a prescription.

It's easy enough to manage without loo rolls (just dig out some old newspapers, which are perfectly well suited to the task) but it's not so easy to find back-up solutions for essential medicines.

This is another way in which the conspirators will kill off the sick and the elderly – the prime targets for their on-going programme of domestic genocide.

And it also helps strengthen the social credit programme.

If you aren't considered a 'good' person you won't be allowed access to medicines of any kind.

Micro-aggression

You'd have thought there were enough intolerant people around.

Wearing the standard uniform of the woke (Lycra bicycle shorts and a helmet with a camera attached) armies of pettifogging bullies are constantly on alert, forever waiting to be offended. These are the people who regard multiculturalism as a religion and patriotism as a crime.

Someone decided that Black Lives Matter, 'Me-too', political correctness, positive discrimination and so on weren't causing enough pain, and so 'micro-aggression' was invented.

What this means, I think, is that we aren't being sensitive enough, and we aren't complaining enough. We should look around more to find little things that sort of upset us a soupcon. Apparently, we need to find more people to blame.

So, for example, we have to learn to be offended when people say simple things like 'That's a nice hat', 'Where are you going on holiday this year?' and 'Thank you for the birthday card'. And we have to be deeply hurt when people fail to open a door for us (even if they are 100 yards away at the time) or buy an ice cream and fail to buy one for everyone else in the queue.

You can see where this is heading, can't you?

There will be lots more complaints to the 'authorities', lots more arrests and lots more deducted social credit points. And the strange thing is that no tribe in history has been as intolerant as these intolerant battalions of miseries. These professional whingers do not accept that other people are entitled to hold views that are different to their own and they will 'cancel' and 'no platform' anyone who dares to express an independent opinion. (The cancel culture doesn't just apply to comedians. It also complains to truth-telling doctors and scientists. I doubt if anyone has been cancelled or de-platformed more than I have.)

Life is going to get wonderful for the conspirators and really tedious for the rest of us.

Migration Policies

The conspirators have enthusiastically encouraged migration for many years. Their aim is to break up nationalities and communities and to destroy patriotism.

People have been pouring out of the UK in hundreds of thousands (but nowhere near as fast as people have been pouring in). The emigrants are quitting the UK because they can see that things are going to hell in a handcart and they want to get out and find something better.

Unfortunately, the bad news is that the conspirators are operating globally and so packing up your stuff and moving to another country isn't going to be much help, unless you are simply looking for somewhere with nicer weather (which is why government spokesmen always say people emigrate from the UK).

New World Order

The New World Order is already here. We're living in it. And things are going to get far, far worse during the coming months because we are now already in the kill phase of the Great Reset. Decisions are made by, or according to the demands of, a tiny group of lobbyists and cultists who have been manipulated into representing the interests of the conspirators – either wittingly or though stupidity and ignorance.

We are being controlled by conspirators who control the sort of people who believe that gluing themselves to the road in front of ambulances is a good thing to do.

The world is full of people who think that those of us who worry about what is happening are half crazed conspiracy theorists. But the odd thing is that most of those people who think we are conspiracy theorists are themselves concerned about things that are happening and that have affected them. The problem is that they haven't looked at the big picture – they don't realise that all the bad things that have been happening in the last few years are connected. The rebranded flu, global warming, the manipulated war against Russia, the war against us, the deliberately destroyed global economy, the price rises, the inflation – they are all linked.

The innocents have failed to put two and two together, partly because they've been too busy worrying about individual threats to their daily lives, partly because they find it difficult to believe that anyone could conceive of a plot as evil as the one that has been underway for years, partly because they're naïve, unquestioning and too ready to believe what they're told by an utterly corrupt mainstream media, and partly because right from the start those of us who've told the truth have been demonised, lied about, censored, suppressed and very effectively silenced by the mainstream media.

When the Great Reset finally arrives, Sir Klaus Schwab, knighted by Queen Elizabeth for services to conspiracy, will be the unelected King of an entirely corrupt world government. Schwab, a 40s villain from central casting, a cross between Dr Strangelove, Ernst Blofeld and Dr Mengele, will be surrounded by a gang of C list crooks, conspirators and half-forgotten celebrities.

If we're not careful we are going to be controlled by those I regard as sad, sorry, second-rate human beings; people such as Fauci, Whitty, shabby little civil servants, and Gates, a friend of Jeffrey Epstein and the BBC. (If Epstein were still alive, the BBC would doubtless give him a chat show.) Dolly Parton and Piers Morgan will be joint Global Ministers in charge of apparently knowing everything but, in reality, understanding nothing. Charles, a 70 odd year old bloke who has to have help taking the top off his breakfast egg and putting toothpaste on his brush, will be in charge of entitlement with William and Kate, a pair of Stepford wives, as his assistants. The Duke and Duchess of California will doubtless be in charge of whingeing and sulking – and a good job they'll make of it I'm sure.

If we allow these sad and sorry creatures to defeat us it will be like the Brazilian football team being thrashed by a team of one-legged pirates with the scurvy.

Oil and Gas Prices

If the idiotic climate change cultists get their way everything is going to stop working and most of us are going to die, cold and hungry.

Bullied, pushed and conned by insane global warming cultists, governments everywhere are promising to do away with fossil fuels. There is much talk of oil and gas being left in the ground, unused and unwanted.

But fossil fuels satisfy most of our energy supply.

Wind power and solar polar are unreliable and inefficient and they provide only a tiny percentage of our energy needs. Biomass (by far the greatest source of so-called renewable energy) is worse for the environment than coal. All those trees have to be chopped down, cut up, moved around in lorries, loaded onto ships and then transported vast distances before they are burnt to create electricity. Biomass is neither efficient nor environmentally sound.

Other 'alternative' fuels are equally useless.

Hydrogen is no more than a joke since it is made using fossil fuels.

Nuclear energy is sound, clean and surprisingly safe but the greens don't like it, and it takes at least ten years to build a functioning nuclear power plant, so we can discount nuclear power for the near future.

That leaves us dependent for the foreseeable future on oil, gas and (dare I mention it) coal.

The oil and gas industries have been demonised for some years now. Pension funds and investment funds have been bullied by noisy pressure groups, into not investing in them. Banks have been pressured into not lending money to companies exploring for new supplies. Oil and gas companies have been harassed and vilified. As a result exploration for new supplies of oil and gas has slowed dramatically.

In 2014, companies spent $900 billion a year looking for oil and gas. Today they spend around a third of that.

The same thing has happened to coal – even though many countries, particularly China, are busy building new coal fired plants.

Despite all the protests and the pressure groups, our consumption of oil, gas and coal isn't going down. The world still runs almost entirely on energy derived from fossil fuels. And this isn't going to change for generations to come, though the oil fields which have supplied us in the past are running out and are not being replaced.

The result is that oil and gas prices are going to continue to soar for years to come. Oh, of course, they will go up and down. But the trend will be upwards.

Oh, and the price of electricity will continue to soar.

Why is electricity going to be more expensive?

That's simple.

Most of it is produced from fossil fuels or (as is the case with biomass) cannot be obtained, transported and used without fossil fuels.

One Party State

Millions of people must by now have noticed that there really isn't much difference between the various political parties.

In the UK, the three main parties (the Conservative Party, the Labour Party and the Liberal Democrats) have largely interchangeable policies and believe in the same future for mankind as the Communist Party. They all believe the global warming myth. They all believe that there was a genuine pandemic in the world in 2020 and 2021. They all believe that it was essential that Britain became involved in Russia's invasion of Ukraine and they believe in the New World Order, the Great Reset and social credit. (The Greens offer oddball policies for Guardian reading school teachers and there are one or two absurd nationalist parties promoting independence).

This is no accident.

The one party state is a prelude to our abandoning whatever remains of our democracy. If we have no reason to vote, and little interest in the outcome of elections, then we will be far more ready to accept an unelected world government.

Online Safety Bills

All around the world governments are introducing what they call 'online safety bills'.

These pieces of legislation are promoted, and sold to the public, as though they are designed to protect free speech, to punish trolls, terrorists and mad extremists and to protect internet users from misinformation and disinformation.

In fact, of course, the bills aren't designed to protect ordinary internet users from abuse, they aren't going to get rid of anonymous trolls and they won't stop spamming and all the various frauds which have made the internet a dangerous place for people to explore.

These bills are designed to do away with freedom of speech, to suppress truth-tellers, to silence anyone questioning the official government line on any subject, to get rid of privacy, to control discussion, to remove debate and to punish platforms and writers who dare to publish anything questioning the Google approved garbage pouring out of drug companies, government advisors, paid and bought for scientists and doctors and crooked politicians. Only communists and other left wing cultists should welcome this legislation which is in reality a charter for deceivers and propagandists. The conspirators are creating a world that would shock even Stalin in its lack of humanity.

Opposition Research

When political parties, conglomerates and lobbyists want to attack their critics, or the opposition, they do research designed to help them discredit them. When they can't find anything they just make things up, distort truths, misquote, lie and remove from the record anything which might be considered to add to the opposition's credibility.

That is what the conspirators have been doing for two years. They have done everything possible to destroy the credibility of any significant opponent with any medical or scientific training.

The conspirators have been aided in their aims by huge internet sites such as Google, YouTube, Facebook, Twitter and Wikipedia and by a small army of professionals working for organisations such as the SIS, the CIA and the British Army. (The British Army, paid for by taxpayers, has a special propaganda unit, the 77th Brigade, which seems to me to exist to use psy-op tricks to suppress the truth and demonise truth-tellers).

Passports

Like many civil servants in other departments, a number of passport office staff in Britain (including the boss) have been reported to be working from home.

Coincidentally, some would-be travellers trying to renew their passports had to wait ten weeks for what appears to be an apparently simple and straightforward transaction to be completed.

Citizens have reported having to wait for hours for someone to answer the phone.

Why the passport office staff have been working from home is, on the face of it, difficult to understand.

It is difficult to think of a department where attendance at an office is more crucial. Old passports are posted in to an office. New passports must be posted out. How anyone with functioning neurones can possibly think that the passport office can be managed by people working from home is difficult to understand. Are the passport office staff really sorting out piles of new passports on their kitchen tables?

(Incidentally, much the same sort of delays were encountered by motorists wanting to renew their driving licences. The staff responsible for the distribution of driving licences were also said to be working from home. Again, it was always clear that this wouldn't work. Indeed, civil servants at the Driver and Vehicle Licensing Agency were paid in full to stay at home and do no work. The result was what the backlog for issuing licences for car and lorry drivers rose to 1.6 million. Despite this the stay-at-home and do-no-work staff were given nearly £2.2 million in performance bonuses. And delays through another agency mean that those wanting to take a driving test may have to wait ten months for a test.)

The passport confusion has been enhanced by the fact that instead of a British passport being renewed from the expiry of the old document, a passport is now renewed from the date of application. This means that passport holders who apply early will lose months of passport validity and the passport office will pull in more money.

The chaos caused by all this nonsense will obviously help cut international travel.

And this, of course, is part of the plan.

In the future, only those who have a satisfactory social credit score, and are entitled to fast track their passport application and renewal, will be entitled to travel.

Pensions

The only people immune to the incompetence of the central bankers are the central bankers themselves. The Bank of England specialises at screwing up the economy, and it is the fault of the people who work there that inflation is now soaring while interest rates are still at an all-time low. However, as I have pointed out elsewhere in this book, the 5,500 retired members of the Bank of England's pension fund don't have to worry about low interest rates or high inflation. The Bank's staff are to receive a pension increase of over 11% this summer. I doubt if there are any pensioners in the country who are treated as lavishly and as over-generously as this bunch of useless quarter-witted numbskulls whose collective incompetence will impoverish generations of tax payers. To put this unwarranted largesse in perspective, I would point out that because I worked as a doctor in hospitals and general practice, and paid some of my earnings into the NHS scheme, I have a small NHS pension which will rise by 3.1% in the coming year. My state pension will also rise by 3.1%.

Police

In May 2022, the UK's new chief inspector of constabulary felt it necessary to tell the nation's police forces that they are not 'the thought police'. The inspector also reminded the police that 'different thoughts' are not an offence. It seems unlikely that the police in general will take notice of this.

Judges have also expressed concern about the way the police have been operating, pointing out that the 25,000 non-crime hate incidents recorded annually by the police have risked interfering with people's right to express their opinions.

In 2022, a police officer in Merseyside put up a billboard wrongly stating that 'being offensive is an offence'.

Politicians

There is an extraordinarily widespread myth, believed by millions, that most of the people who run countries are well-intentioned, compassionate, well-informed and honourable as well as committed to caring for the citizens they have sworn to protect.

In fact, of course, the vast majority of politicians are selfish, dangerous and crooked. No other group of professionals (not even lawyers) see as many of their number imprisoned each year as do politicians.

Politicians are, as a breed, controlled by lobbyists (who are, by definition, bought and paid for) and advisors (who are too frequently operating on behalf of previous or future employers).

And so for the last few years our politicians have been working for the conspirators. Some of them are members of the conspiracy, of course, but even the ones who aren't are guided by advisors who are. As they always have done, politicians always follow the money.

Today, there is no incentive for anyone to vote since in most countries (most notably the UK) there is no discernible difference between the main political parties. They are all sharing the same false fears and offering the same fake solutions.

This is exactly what the conspirators want, of course.

In the medium to long term, the men in expensive suits, the conspirators, don't want popular governments.

Look at what is happening around the world.

Prime Ministers and Presidents everywhere are hated. The ones who win elections only ever gain a minority of the vote.

It's pretty well impossible to think of a political leader anywhere in the world who would win a popularity contest.

And that is the plan.

The billionaire conspirators controlling our present and future are deliberately doing everything they can to ensure that political leaders everywhere are hated.

And then the people of the world will jump at the chance of a World Government run by fresh, unknown, friendly faces – bringing promises of peace, harmony and prosperity.

And the people will be so pleased to see the back of their despised politicians that they won't really notice that they have become slaves within the New World Order.

A final thought.

The aim of politicians these days (which is to say, of course, the aim of the conspirators preparing us for the Great Reset and a life of social credit) is to divide us.

By dividing us, and encouraging us to fight one another, the politicians (that is to say the conspirators) turn us into warring tribes, and distract us from any thought that we might unite to defend ourselves against the Great Reset and social credit.

And so politicians encourage us to be outraged, utterly outraged, at any slight we might notice. Ethnic groups are pitted against one another. The young are taught to loathe and despise the elderly and the elderly are encouraged to despise and loathe the millennials and those who have followed them. And, of course men are taught that women are the enemy because women are taught that men are the enemy.

There was a time when I would have honoured to welcome the Prime Minister into my home. If a member of the Cabinet, or a member of the royal family had knocked on the door and asked to borrow a cup of sugar I had have gladly helped them out, and told them to keep the cup. These days if any politician or member of the royal family knocked on the door I'd rush upstairs, open a window and tip boiling tar over them.

Population Control

On April 1st, 2019 the United Nations member states agreed to implement their plans on population and development.

The plans included massive controls on population growth – targeting in particular Asia and Africa. And the elderly and the sick will be culled.

The aim is to cut the world's population from 7.5 billion to 500 million.

Privacy

Privacy is a long cherished principle. The English used to talk of their home being their castle. Libel laws were designed to help us protect our reputations.

In the New Normal, after the Great Reset is established, the power will all be given to international companies run by billionaires and those international companies will use governments as their enforcers.

In his prophetic book '1984', George Orwell wrote that man exerts power over others by making them suffer. 'Power is inflicting pain and humiliation,' he wrote. 'Unless he is suffering how can you know that he is obeying your will and not his own?'

We will be expected to give up our privacy for convenience and we will enter a world of constant surveillance. This is already happening, of course. Smart speakers in phones, television sets, thermostats, fridges and so on have microphones. Those who fill their houses with wonderful internet linked equipment (door bells, vacuum cleaners, watches, lawn mowers, security systems, bathroom scales, microwave ovens, thermostats, CD players and so on are living in homes full of Peeping Toms. Orwell worried about what he called 'telescreens' – television screens which watch us while we watch what they show. This is exactly what has happened. Our televisions can listen to us and they can watch us. (We have remarkably little spy equipment in our house but last night I mentioned to Antoinette that I thought we had a patch of mould in the house. This morning I looked at the internet and I was swamped with advertisements from companies dealing with mould.)

And even when internet platforms claim to be protecting us, they probably aren't. In May 2022, Twitter settled a $150 million regularly lawsuit over claims it harvested the phone numbers of 140 million users 'as a security feature' but secretly used the information it had obtained for targeting adverts instead. The US Federal Trade Commission commented: 'If you're struck by the irony of a company exploiting consumers' privacy concerns in a way that facilitated further invasions of customers' privacy, it's an irony not lost on the FTC.'

When he came to power in the US, Obama promised an open and transparent government. But in a single year his administration classified 77.5 million documents. In 'Deadly Deception Exposed', Soren Roest Korsgaard reports that although Obama received the peace prize in 2009, in 2016 alone his administration dropped at least 26,171 bombs in Iraq, Syria, Afghanistan, Libya, Yemen, Somalia and Pakistan. Wedding parties, funerals, children's soccer game, hospitals, schools, farmers working and citizens walking peacefully in their streets were all killed by Obama bombs. US Governments have so far spent $6 trillion on wars in Iraq and Afghanistan alone.

Microphones in television sets, computers and (of course) mobile phones of all kinds pick up everything you talk about. It is because of this (as much as because of the searches you make) that advertisers can recommend specific products which they hope you will buy. Search engines such as Google and social media sites such as Facebook have totally betrayed the interests of consumers, too many of whom still think that 'free' comes without surprises.

Major companies such as Google can control the information we see by labelling the truth as misinformation and by censoring and hiding websites which they consider 'inappropriate'. Between 80% and 93% of online searches are done through that one company (when did monopolies become acceptable?) and Google can and does influence behaviour by promoting fear and false narratives. Not surprisingly, since they're part of the same company, YouTube does the same – promoting videos which are considered useful and eliminating, censoring, banning or removing anything which contains truths considered inconvenient by the conspirators. I had well over 100 videos removed from YouTube though not one of them contained anything inaccurate.

Progress

The Victorian Age gave Britain great bridges, a terrific railway system, an efficient sewage system, fresh running water in every home, well designed hospitals (built on the excellent Nightingale system) and the best education system in the world.

The Victorian Age is widely derided today.

The Elizabethan age of Queen Elizabeth II gave us unsafe, wobbly bridges, an inefficient and overpriced railway system, undrinkable drinking water, crumbling sewage systems (with untreated sewage dumped straight into rivers and the sea), hospitals which kill more people than they save, a medical system comparable with that of the Middle Ages, an education system which has given us a nation of illiterate, innumerate bigots, who have firmly ill-founded opinions on global warming but who demand to be driven when they want to be 100 yards away from where they are sitting.

And we've had a queen and royal family who have espoused political causes (such as vaccination and global warming) but never stood up for the people who pay their extortionate wages. The royals have made a lot of noise about global warming but they never said a word when elderly people, who had been loyal for decades, were slaughtered in nursing homes.

It all seems chaotic and a result of incompetence.

But it isn't.

It's all planned.

It is the planned obsolescence of the human species.

Recycling

Recycling was introduced, worldwide, as a tool to teach citizens to become compliant. Forcing citizens to sort their rubbish into up to nine separate bags or boxes every week had absolutely nothing to do with 'saving the planet' and everything to do with teaching citizens (through a mixture of fines and shame) to behave 'responsibly' i.e. to do as they were told without looking too closely at the rationale of what they were being told to do.

The recycling never had anything to do with protecting the planet, of course. Most of the rubbish sorted, washed and collected in the UK was taken abroad, by lorry or ship or train, and burnt or dumped. It was, quite simply, impractical and not cost effective to recycle the material that had been collected. And, of course, collecting the sorted rubbish involved massive costs in terms of cash and pollution.

Today, the recycling business has reached an apogee of lunacy. Councils introduce ever more complex rules and fees. They refuse to take away much of the waste that is collected. And those wanting to take their rubbish to a 'recycling' centre will probably have to make an appointment and answer a host of questions. It is no surprise that fly-tipping has become a major problem. The biggest causes of plastic in the sea are dumped fishing gear and plastic waste (much of it officially designated as recycled) which has been dumped by ships.

The good news, however, is that in Britain, recycling rates are falling. More and more people have become aware that the whole recycling movement was just another piece of manipulative trickery.

Re-wilding

At the same time as controls are being introduced on most animals (on the grounds that they transmit diseases to humans) and millions of farm animals are being culled , the British Government has committed itself (and the British people) to set aside 30% of the nation's land and seas for nature conservancy by the year 2030.

By the sort of strange coincidence that we are now getting used to, exactly the same thing is happening everywhere in the world.

These vast tracts of land and sea won't be playgrounds or farms. They will be monitored, protected areas – with enforcement agencies present to make sure that members of the public don't go onto the land. And to make certain that we don't trespass on these new forbidden areas, wolves, lynx, wild boar and bison are being released.

All this will cost huge sums of money and, on an already overcrowded island, it will dramatically reduce the amount of land available for farming, parks, sports and enjoyment. England is already one of the most crowded countries on earth and as immigrants pour in and more land is taken out of use, so the overcrowding will get worse.

Farmers aren't complaining about the loss of useable land because for some years now they have been paid huge sums of money to do absolutely nothing with their land. This absurdly wasteful programme, organised by the European Union, is called 'setaside' and the aim, apparently, is to reduce crop surpluses.

The aim of all this, of course, is to reduce the amount of land available for productive farming and to reduce the amount of home-grown food for sale.

Reducing the amount of farm-grown food available will make the population reliant on laboratory and factory grown food, the distribution and control of which will be far easier to manage.

The medium to long-term aim is to control food stocks so that those who have unsatisfactory social credit scores can be prevented from buying food for themselves and their families.

Royal Family

I used to be a royalist. I thought they earned their keep by attracting foreign tourists. And I thought their presence in our constitution saved us from having a dictator.

But that was long ago. No more.

Now I believe that sensible folk should boo and hiss whenever they see a member of the royal family. They should wave two fingers, rather than hands, flags or embroidered hankies. The modern royals exhibit greed, self-importance, hubris, selfishness and hypocrisy but absolutely no sense of responsibility, loyalty or respect towards the people who pay for their rock-star lifestyles.

On Thursday 25th February 2021, the queen of England called millions of people selfish because they refuse to take an experimental, untested, unnecessary and deadly jab. She's either an unbelievably ignorant, batty old crone or part of the lying, evil cabal determined to take over the world and kill millions of us. I'm betting on the latter.

To say that the jab didn't hurt was, quite possibly, the most patronising and pathetic thing I've ever heard anyone say.

Does she not realise that most people are more likely to die in an accident while heading for the vaccination centre than they are to die of the rebranded flu?

The queen says she felt protected because she had (allegedly) been injected with the covid jab. How mad is this bloody woman? Even the WHO won't promise that the jab will stop anyone getting or spreading the rebranded flu.

Britain's royal family has played an enthusiastic part in the plan to make the British people accept Agenda 21.

Hypocrite Prince Charles has for many years been a keen advocate of the global warming myth, busily flying around the world to attend global warming conferences. Charles's two sons, William and Harry have also been keen supporters of the same myth and have spent much of their lives flying around the world to prove their contempt for the mad theory they pretend to espouse.

Members of the royal family also claim the world is overpopulated but breed like lusty teenage tarts who haven't heard of contraception. There are now so many members of the royal family that the massive balcony at Buckingham Palace isn't big enough to hold them all. When he was alive, Prince Philip said that he wanted to come back as a deadly virus to reduce the population.

Queen Elizabeth II did a good deal of waving and shaking during the active years of her reign but did very little of value. Her main contribution has been to produce four of the most entirely foul and useless human beings in history. Her family make the Borgias look loveable.

The astonishing thing about Charles is the hubris, the certainty that he, a man who has never known any of the normal worries of the world, an intensely over-privileged member of an arrogant and over privileged family, thinks he knows best how the world should be managed.

He, like the rest of his family, has betrayed the British people and the people of the Commonwealth.

His son, the Duke of Cambridge is also blessed with copious quantities of hubris and appears to be a world class hypocrite. He has stated that there are too many people in the world – but he has three children. He flies constantly but claims that the myth of 'global warming is irrefutable'. Just how or why he knows this to be the case, he has not bothered to share with us. As always with the royal family it is a case of 'do as I say, not as I do'.

If the royals understand that the myth of global warming was devised as an excuse for the Great Reset then they are traitors. If they don't understand then they are gullible fools.

We should get rid of the existing royal family completely. We can confiscate their estates and, since the royals are too incompetent to earn a living, provide them with modest, rented accommodation on the top floor of a high rise block of flats.

But that would leave us with the danger of having a power mad president and so, to avoid that dire eventuality, we should have rotating royals. This could be arranged via a weekly lottery. Punters entering the lottery could have a chance to be king or queen for a week.

The temporary holders of the royal offices would do the usual hand waving and opening of cupboards, envelopes and approved buildings – and then, at the end of their week, go back to their usual lives. The confiscated royal estates could be used to fund this simple operation so there would be no drain on taxpayers.

Candidates for the role should be stupid, vacuous, vain and have a grotesque sense of entitlement. Almost any successful reality television 'stars' would be suitable for these roles.

Savers

Savers are being attacked by a twin combination of high inflation and low interest rates. Both these are deliberate. The aim, of course, is to impoverish the thrifty and reduce individual independence. The aim (in the immortal words of the World Economic Forum) is for us all to 'own nothing' because only then will we be 'happy'. Those who fail the social credit test for a weekly government hand-out will either be reduced to begging on the streets or confined to a poor house or debtors' prison as described by Charles Dickens.

Search Engines

When Google started life, the company motto was 'do no evil'. I wonder if they were serious. The motto certainly didn't last long.

Today, Google controls 97% of internet searches done on mobile phones and it is the most evil company on the planet – surpassing even Monsanto and Goldman Sachs in the harm it does. Google, which effectively has a monopoly, spends around $1 billion a year and earns $100 billion.

Google is supposed to be a search engine but it manipulates searches, promotes fake experts, suppresses, demonises and libels honest experts and buries search results which it considers inconvenient. Google long ago betrayed its promises and searches are dominated by advertised and sponsored sites. The information provided by Google (a good deal of it taken from the unreliable site Wikipedia) is low quality and does more harm than good. Google is responsible for brain washing, controlling elections and fixing public policy. Its associate YouTube does the same thing. It is ironic that the big tech companies, often described as 'disruptive', should do everything in their power to suppress original thought.

Through its association with Wikipedia, Google makes sure that bad people are eulogised and truth-tellers are demonised.

Does Google make the decisions about what to push and what to hide and who to promote and who to destroy? I very much doubt it. Google simple does what it is told to do by the conspirators.

Shops

The closure of bricks and mortar shops (large and small) may appear to be an unforeseen consequence of the lockdowns and the economic downturn which followed. But the damage done to economies everywhere was deliberately exaggerated by financial policies (followed worldwide) which were designed either by incompetent buffoons or by evil people pretending to be incompetent buffoons.

The deliberately planned consequence will be that most or all of our shopping will in future be done online. We will, therefore, travel less. We will spend less time out of our homes. And our buying will be checked and controlled by the conspirators. They will see exactly what we buy.

Those who have poor social credit ratings will be very limited in what they are allowed to buy.

Smart Meters

In the UK, citizens are not allowed to buy their electricity at the cheapest rates unless they have a smart meter fitted.

There is absolutely no sensible reason for this other than control.

Snitches and Sneaks

We already live in the age of the snitch and the sneak. Governments everywhere are constantly bringing in new laws to encourage people to 'tell' on their friends, neighbours and workmates. The aim, of course, is to ensure that none of us trusts anyone else.

And in this new world of course, it only takes one complaint to produce a result.

A hotel I enjoyed visiting because it had a huge open fireplace with crackling logs burning throughout the winter got rid of its open fire and replaced it with a log burner – with the doors always safely shut. The manager told me that the local council had received one complaint from a visitor who felt that it was dangerous to have an open fireplace. And so, on instructions from a man (or woman) in a cheap suit, the hotel had installed the log burner.

A church where bells have rung out for 500 years had to stop all bell ringing after the local council received a single complaint from someone who had bought a house within earshot of the bells.

A motor racing circuit which had held meetings for half a century, had to dramatically limit its events because of a newcomer to the area had complained to the council about the noise.

General speaking, if a complaint supports the general aims of the Great Reset then a single complaint will be quite sufficient to be effective. On the other hand, if a thousand protestors complain about some aspect of the Great Reset, their complaints will be ignored, dismissed or filed as irrelevant and merely troublesome. Indeed, protestors who complain about aspects of the Great Reset are quite likely to find themselves reported to the police, their professional or trade organisation or their employers.

In the future the snitches and sneaks will be everywhere, making personal judgements and telephoning the police.

Indeed, the sneaks are already everywhere – they can now download an App onto their smart phones to use as a speed camera. I hope those who use it learn to polish their boots and click their heels.

In the May 11, 2022 edition of a magazine called Country Life I read this: 'Anyone who feels concerned about potential fire risks, for example (because they see) people using a BBQ in an area where they shouldn't be, should call the police on the non-emergency number 101,' says James Herd, director of reserves management at Surrey Wildlife Trust.

Passers-by who do this will doubtless receive bonus marks for their social credit score.

For some years now, lawyers and accountants have been legally obliged to report their clients to the authorities if they suspect them of committing, or having committed, any sort of crime. If the lawyer or accountant warns the client that what they are doing may or will result in their being reported, then the lawyer or accountant will themselves be guilty of a serious crime and be sent to prison.

The tax authorities use snitches too and I know of situations where people under investigation have managed to close their own investigations by giving the tax inspector someone else's name as a possibly better target for investigation.

Social Media

The conspirators have used social media ruthlessly to divide people and to create anger, depression, anxiety and violence. Professional influencers make fortunes promoting products and the insane gather vast readerships by offering increasingly outrageous views. Eager would-be stars and C list celebrities photograph themselves in bizarre costumes or situations designed solely to gather attention. The sites have become a working place for exhibitionists and megalomaniacs. But it is the way that the big sites (such as Facebook and Twitter) censor users which has created fear and done most damage to society.

The authorities could have done more to control social media more effectively, and prevented the chaos and pain. They could, for example, have forced the big sites to do away with anonymity (the essential tool of the psychopathic trolls who cause 95% of the pain and distress). But that would not have suited the conspirators' plan.

Tourism

One of the big aims of the Great Reset is to control the amount that people travel. The conspirators want people (or, at least, the relatively few who will be left) to do far less travelling.

This has nothing to do with global warming (which the conspirators know is a hoax because they are responsible for having created the hoax).

The conspirators want us to travel less for two reasons.

First, they know that the amount of oil left on earth is running out. We long ago reached peak oil. (If you want to know more about this take a look at my book 'A Bigger Problem than Climate Change: The End of Oil' which may shock you.)

Second, controlling the amount that people travel will help give the controllers of the social credit system a quick easy way to control behaviour.

It is partly because of this desire to cut the amount of travel that is done that local councils (invariably controlled by the usual suspects from the World Economic Forum and Common Purpose) are doing everything they can to make visits to their town as unpleasant as possible.

In the spring of 2022, councils all over the country suddenly put up car park prices by massive amounts. Many town councils actually doubled the fees they charge – making town car parks as expensive as airport parking lots.

Loos were closed in many towns, to deter visitors, and in towns where a loo remained open, charges were introduced. For example, the Cornish seaside resort of St Ives, which relies on tourism for its survival, announced in May 2022 that it intended to start charging tourists and the owners of holiday homes to use any of its public lavatories. Only local residents would be able to use the loos freely. Visitors had to use a bank card or a smartphone or by buy a pre-payment card in advance. There is no talk yet of the number of sheets of loo paper being controlled but I expect that will happen.

This is a perfect example of social credit in practice.

(I'm pleased to say that this crude plan will probably backfire. A few years ago St Ives tried to stop people buying second homes in the town, but study by the London School of Economics found that the ban had led to a reduction in the number of available homes because building companies went elsewhere. The result was that the competition for housing increased.)

Elsewhere, in England, local councils are advertising 'a unique opportunity for community groups and local businesses to creatively repurpose public toilet premises'.

The conspirators themselves, of course, will not be in any way inconvenienced by any of this.

Have you noticed how many billionaire Bilderberger conspirators now have huge yachts? It's no coincidence. The conspirators haven't all suddenly become enthusiastic deep sea fishermen or Jet-ski aficionados. As the world falls apart, in the preparation for the Great Reset, the conspirators clearly plan to live on their super yachts. These big boats have desalination plants, windmills and solar power. Most important of all they can be fuelled and stocked with food while still at sea. The billionaire owners will not need to approach land at all.

One of the reasons for pushing up the price of oil has always been to preserve as much oil as possible for the private aeroplanes, yachts and toys belonging to the billionaire conspirators. They are well aware that the world's supply of oil is running out – and they want to keep as much of it as they can for themselves. Those super-yachts use a great amount of diesel.

Trans-humanism

Trans-humanism isn't just about turning people into robots; it is also about what the conspirators call 'human enhancement technologies';

it is about collecting and manipulating the information people receive; it is about implanting devices which can be used to control the brain; it is about mass formation psychosis, concentrating on specific subjects – the essence of totalitarian thinking.

The conspirators say that they want to put implants into brains in order to enable the paralysed and the silent to walk and to communicate.

But, I fear, those are merely the selling points for an evil process of control. They openly boast about improving the human mind.

Trans-humanism is an essential part of the Great Reset, and the conspirators openly talk about hacking into the human body and using DNA 'improving' technology to create more capable humans. Trans-humanism is about engineering people to fit the aims of the conspirators.

And to keep the conspirators alive forever, they talk of using 3D printers to make new, better, stronger human organs such as hearts, kidneys, lungs and livers.

It is worth remembering that in January 1961, President Dwight D. Eisenhower's farewell address to the American nation didn't just warn of the unwarranted influence of the military-industrial complex. President Eisenhower also warned that public policy could be captured by elite scientists and technologists. He would, perhaps, be shocked but not surprised to see that faceless and unelected people now talk glibly about digital ID, blockchain, cryptocurrencies, nanontechnology, graphene oxide, 5G, cloning and social credit.

Virtue Signalling

The epidemic of maskitis which has enveloped the world for the last two years has not been cured. In many countries around the world, a high percentage of people are still wearing their face coverings in the street and in shops and supermarkets.

Why are so many people ignoring the danger to their own health?

I don't believe they are still scared. Some (mostly women) wear them so that they don't have to bother with make-up. Some wear them because they know they're plug ugly and the face covering gives them a chance to hide their ugliness from the world. Some wear them because they bought a pile of them cheap from a stall on the market and don't want them to go to waste. Some have face coverings that match their outfit and they'd now feel improperly dressed without a face covering.

But I think the majority of them are virtue signalling numpties. 'Look at me, I'm such a good person that I'm wearing a face covering even though I know I don't have to.' You can see it in their eyes: the superciliousness; the sense of moral superiority.

The virtue signalling started with recycling. The illiterate buffoons who accepted the lies about recycling, who washed out their bottles and yoghurt cartons with precious water and sorted their rubbish into six, seven, eight nine different piles, became the obedient wearers of face coverings. It was a training process to turn people into zombies.

The people wearing face coverings are the people who buy electric cars. They buy the wretched things because they think that driving an electric car makes them look like good people. If they could read and had the brains of a pea they'd know that electric cars are worse for the environment than diesel and petrol driven cars. And they should know (but probably don't) that the electricity that drives their tin cans is produced by burning bits of chopped up tree.

Now, the obedient, virtue signalling numpties are wearing little ribbons to show that they support Ukraine and hate Russia and all Russians. They're filling boxes with tins and packets of almost out of date food (that they've decided they don't like) and they are taking their boxes along to special centres in the vain and stupid belief that their goodies will stop the war. Do they think the Ukrainians are going to throw tins of beans at the Russians? Do they have any idea how much it costs to sort and transport a box of unwanted food to Ukraine?

Worse still, the virtue signalling numpties want all contact with Russia to be stopped. They want Russians to be fired and expelled from whatever country they are living in. And they want governments to stop buying Russian oil, gas, wheat and metals. Isn't that racism?

Did the virtue signalling numpties behave this way during any one of the other wars that have been conducted in recent years? Iraq?

Kuwait? Kosovo? Syria? Yemen? Ethiopia? Sudan? What about when Russia invaded Ukraine a few years ago?

There are wars going on all over the world – particularly in Africa. But the only war the virtue signallers care about is the one they've been told to care about.

What about the huge numbers of people the West killed in Iraq? What about Guantanamo Bay? Obama promised to close it on his first day in office. Eight years later it was still there. I don't see anyone protesting about that? What about the rendition of untried prisoners?

Are the virtue signalling numpties really so stupid that they don't realise that their actions will prolong the war and result in hundreds of millions of deaths from starvation in Africa? Do they not realise that they're doing exactly what the billionaire conspirators want them to do?

The virtue signallers don't realise that they have become collaborators in the greatest and most evil conspiracy the world has ever seen.

The selfish, sanctimonious Ukraine supporting collaborators are part of a new plague: the plague of virtue signallers.

And this is a plague that could destroy us all in the end.

Working from Home

One of the many absurd rules brought in during the Government generated hysteria over the 2020 edition of the common or garden flu, was that millions of people were told to work from home. Bus drivers, train drivers and those employed to unblock drains were allowed to go to work as normal. Everyone else simply sat down at their kitchen table, pushed aside the breakfast things and plugged in the laptop and pretended to work. Huge numbers of people discovered something called 'zoom' which enabled them to have face to face meeting with their office colleagues.

Not surprisingly, this new way of working proved very popular. Office workers, such as civil servants, didn't have to get dressed, drive to the railway station, stand in a grubby train for an hour and struggle through crowds at their destination station. Instead of buying overpriced coffee and sandwiches, office workers could now make their own coffee and sandwiches. They could make soup for lunch. They could have something on toast. And they didn't really have to do any work at all.

And instead of stretching their legs by going for a walk around the offices occasionally they could take the dog for a walk, prune the roses, go for a bicycle ride, pop next door for a chat or just go back to bed for a snooze.

Very little work got done.

Callers who telephoned their insurance company, the council or the department of something or other would hear the baby and the dog in the background and instead of hearing 'Our lines are very busy at the moment but your call is very important to us' they would be told 'I'm afraid I can't help you with that, I'm working from home and your file is at the office'.

When the rules about not leaving home were eventually lifted, millions decided that they preferred working at home to working at the office.

Civil servants in particular seemed unenthusiastic about ever meeting their colleagues again. Much gibberish was shared about work being a 'state of mind' rather than a 'place' and there were demands to be allowed to continue working from home. Some workers, and civil servants seemed particularly vocal about this, demanded that they be allowed to do their work while abroad. Most workers seemed to prefer the idea of working somewhere sunny with a beach. Oh, and those who had been working in London wanted to continue to receive their special London allowances.

Staff at the Bank of England (either the most corrupt or the most incompetent organisation in the world) were told that they had to go to work just one day a week. The police were said to be working from home. And doctors announced that they too wanted to be able to close their surgeries and consulting rooms and work from home.

There is, of course, always a hidden agenda these days, for the conspirators have thought of everything.

When people work in offices they have a chance to talk to one another. When people travel by train they have a chance to meet and talk to strangers.

But when people work at home they are physically isolated and everything they say is transmitted by telephone or through the internet – with the result that the authorities can hear or see everything that is being discussed.

And there is another reason, too, why working from home is encouraged. (Governments say they are opposed to the idea but they do nothing to force civil servants back to their offices.)

The evidence shows that people who work at home take less exercise (there is no need to walk along the station platform or up and down stairs to another office) and they eat more (with all that food available in the cupboard and in the fridge and in the biscuit barrel it is difficult to escape temptation). There is far more likely to be chocolate available in the average home than in the average office.

Home working will push up the mortality rate.

Office workers who stay at home may think that are in some way free of their bonds but in reality they are less free than they were when they left their homes and went to work.

World Economic Forum

The World Economic Forum used to be a bit of a joke.

Once a year, dictators, presidents and Prime Ministers from around the world would fly to Davos in Switzerland, park their private jets and spend an absolute fortune on vastly overpriced accommodation (at taxpayers' expense) so that they could rub shoulders with self-created, self-lauded celebrities such as Bill Gates, Elon Musk, George Soros, Richard Branson and a variety of other ambitious, company bosses (staying in the same overpriced accommodation but at their shareholders' expense). I suspect that all would be there so that they could have their pictures taken with a pop singer called Bono – the almost inevitable winner of my annual hypocrite of the year for combining an apparent concern for the world's poor with some fancy tax planning that enabled him to avoid paying for his government to do much about the world's poor.

Speakers at the WEF include Xi Jinping, (leader of the Chinese Communist Party), Vladimir Putin (President of Russia), Bill Gates (friend of Jeffrey Epstein and financial partner of the BBC and The Guardian newspaper), Scott Morrison (Australian Premier) and Dr Anthony Fauci (promoter of vaccines). Those attending the annual shindig paid around $50,000 each for a ticket.

The 2022 edition of the shindig was held at the end of May. A spokesman for the WEF boasted that they had over 300 government leaders attending (all at their taxpayer's expense I suspect) including 50 heads of state. The UK was sending someone called Alok Sharma 'to address the climate agenda where Britain has played a leading role'.

The head honcho and chief wizard of the WEF is a scary sounding and even scarier looking bloke called Sir Klaus Schwab, a man who seems to me to have all the solid credibility of a 1960s second hand car salesman working on a bombed site in downtown Birmingham. Schwab was given a knighthood by Queen Elizabeth II for no reason that I can discern other than the theory that she perhaps has a soft spot for foreigners dedicated to conspiracy and totalitarianism. Schwab's background is something of a mystery to me but he appears to have chosen himself to rule the world. He was certainly never elected by any global population that I am aware of – though I suppose it is possible that the world's goblins chose him to be in charge.

But the joke was on us.

The WEF official motto is 'Committed to improving the state of the world' but I doubt if anyone not associated with WEF takes this seriously.

Gradually, over the last 30 years or so the WEF has been planning to take over the world. For all that time they've been running a training programme for young men and women who fancied themselves as world leaders.

In February 2022, the WEF published a new vision for the world. The organisation stated: 'In this Insight Report the World Economic Forum's Taskforce on Data Intermediaries explores the potential to outsource human decision points to an agent acting on an individual's behalf, in the form of a data intermediary. Levers of action for both the public and private sectors are suggested to ensure a future-proof digital policy environment that allows for the seamless and trusted movement of data between people and the technology that serves them.' (I don't think anyone writing documents for the WEF has ever claimed to be better at the English language than they are at understanding humanity, freedom or democracy.)

Once they are through the training programme, the 'graduates' are placed in key positions in governments, the media, finance and technology. I assume that the 'trained' (for which I would like to put 'brainwashed') 'graduates' are found suitable positions by older members of the programme. It's a bit like the freemasons but worse. These Davos men seem to be trained to forget national identities and to think of themselves as global citizens. They are narcissistic, deluded and self-serving megalomaniacs and they seem to me to have been trained to believe that the only thing that matters is the creation of an unelected, globalist government. They are trained to believe that the business interest of the WEF's partners takes precedence over nations and democracies. It's an evil mixture of totalitarianism, fascism and communism. The aim is to get rid of national identities or culture.

I find it difficult to understand what sort of people would want to join such an organisation, which sounds to me like an uncomfortable melange of the Klu Klux Klan, the National Union of Teachers, the Women's Institute and the Hitler Youth programme. I do hope they don't mind my saying that.

I can only assume that the scheme attracts individuals who are not terribly bright, just a percentage point or two above moronic, but nevertheless over-ambitious and ruthlessly self-serving; the sort who were prefects at school; the sort of folk who sneaked to their teachers and later reported the neighbours for putting up a summerhouse in the garden or for burning garden rubbish.

These are people who think that George Orwell's book '1984' is a training manual – and they've been sticking to it very closely. These are mediocre people whose smugness, self-regard and self-righteousness enables them to claim they're making the world a better place because they know better than everyone else what everyone should want and everyone should do. The WEF has bred a small army of Tony Blair clones who have, through contacts with other conspirators, taken over the leadership of many professions, unions, political groups and public bodies. Those leaders have then carried their members with them by a potent mixture of promises, bribery, threats, a sense of entitlement, a generous helping of resentment and some well-orchestrated fake fears.

It seems to me that the aim of the WEF is to do away with democracy, to give total control to the billionaires and to technocrats working in the Deep State. The aim is to hack into people and to remove their free will.

Traditionally, it is said that governments sacrifice the few to protect the lives and interests of the many. In the new world, Schwab's law dictates that the conspirators will sacrifice the many to protect the financial interests of the few – using social credit as the ultimate training and controlling weapon.

The WEF gets its money from a regional partners, industry partner groups and 100 full members or strategic partners. All these companies pay huge chunks of money to the WEF for membership.

The list of partners looks like a compilation of the world's most thoroughly evil companies and, you will not be surprised to hear, the list includes Alphabet (which is Google and YouTube in fancy dress), Meta (the posh name for Facebook), PayPal (busy expelling anyone who dares tell the truth), J.P.Morgan (one of the world's most evil banks) and Goldman Sachs (another one of the world's most evil banks).

The WEF (infamous for its rather threatening, even blood-curdling slogan 'you will own nothing and be happy') is the mastermind behind the Global Reset and works arm in arm with the United Nations to change the world in the way they think it should be.

I believe the WEF is largely behind the jabbing campaigns, the lockdowns, the propaganda, the censorship, the suppression of early medical treatment and the brainwashing and thought control programmes initiated by governments around the world.

Schwab talks with unregulated enthusiasm about brain implants, sensors, artificial intelligence, robots and drones and seems to believe that men and women need the sort of upgrades that only he and his co-conspirators can offer.

I believe the WEF is also behind the targeting and demonization of dissenting physicians.

The overall plan, of course, is to exploit the disruption caused by the three frauds (the covid fraud, the global warming fraud and the war fraud) and to work towards their aim of total control and world domination.

The organisation may sound as if it was dreamt up by Ian Fleming after a few too many drinks but it's all true. You can check it out easily enough.

Who founded it? Well, the boss and face of the WEF is, of course, Sir Klaus Schwab who has been described as 'creepy' and who seems to me to have not been properly glued together.

But just who pulls his strings, and who helped him found the organisation is a mystery. I suspect that Schwab is just a front. The people behind the WEF are rather shy though the names Henry Kissinger, John K. Galbraith and George Soros pop up with monotonous regularity, as do the names Rothschild and Rockefeller. The CIA's fingerprints can be found everywhere. The one certainty is that the long-term plans mean that string pullers are generational controllers – thinking generations ahead.

And the British royal family? Well, I fear that they are far too venal and far too stupid to run anything, but the royals are doubtless involved. There is a picture of a Rothschild prodding Prince Charles in the chest with a stiff finger. It's the sort of gesture a powerful man makes to an underling.

The WEF is not the only organisation with global ambitions. Another rather creepy sounding organisation is called Common Purpose. This too runs training programmes.

World Health Organisation

The World Health Organisation has consistently proved itself to be unreliable, inconsistent and incompetent, and so it is alarming to know that the organisation is proposing a new pandemic treaty which will give it power to force countries and their citizens to do as they are told, if the staff there believe there is a health threat.

There is no doubt that this is the starting point for a world government with a central, unelected body having control over every country in the world. The W.H.O. will have the power to order compulsory lockdowns and forced vaccination programmes. (Self-spreading vaccines are on the way so even those individuals who attempt to defy the W.H.O. will probably find themselves 'vaccinated'.)

If the W.H.O. receives the authority it wants, then an International Health Regulation will empower the WHO director general to declare (on the basis of nothing other than his personal opinion) a health emergency in any country in the world or in all countries in the world. He will have the power to do this regardless of that country's wishes. It will not be necessary for him to produce any evidence whatsoever for his actions. Anyone who tries to oppose whatever action he decides to take will be censored and, no doubt, social credit schemes will be used to punish doubters.

Numerous countries have already announced that they support the plan which takes us straight into the Global Reset, the New World Order, a global dictatorship and an unelected world government.

We must remember that a vaccine promoter called Bill Gates has, without any public votes or public support, but with a good deal of money, succeeded in buying himself effective control of the W.H.O. Gates gave $1 billion to the W.H.O. in 2021 (he is the second largest donor after the United States) and has a massive amount of influence.

The W.H.O, a rancid organisation controlled by the conspirators, has already issued guidance to enable countries to implement digital health passports as recommended by Klaus Schwab and Bill Gates. And digital health passports are, of course, a major step towards control through social credit.

Part Three
So, what do we do?

If we don't defeat the Great Reset, and push back the plan to impose a system of social credit on us all, then we will be the generation who lost control of the world; the generation who gave away our freedom because we were too afraid to fight for it; the generation who betrayed Spartacus. Unless we stop this abomination, man's evolution will go backwards.

If we want to survive we have to prepare for a permanent revolution; we have to fight hard to stop what is happening; we have to fight hard to reverse things that have happened and we have to fight hard to stop things that will happen. If we lose our freedom it will be lost forever.

We need to ignore the distractions, the diversions and the side issues and concentrate on the one, big issue: social credit.

Our fight is a just one and we have Robin Hood and Sir Garwain fighting alongside us, for our cause is just and honourable.

There are, I believe, several things we can do to help ourselves.

First, spread the message from this book as widely as you can. For new information, please visit www.vernoncoleman.com or www.vernoncoleman.org . New material is added most weekdays. Everything is free to download and share and there are no advertisements or sponsors. If you would like to buy a book occasionally it would be much appreciated. (The two sites are similar though www.vernoncoleman.com is more old-fashioned and has been in existence since the 1980s. With two sites running there is a chance that if one is taken down the other will still be there.)

Second, boycott the enemy. Do it legally but don't give money to the BBC. Don't subscribe to Sky. Don't use YouTube or Google – there are other search engines – and if you use Twitter, Facebook or Linkedin remember that you are on enemy territory and beware. These platforms suppress free speech. It's what they do. And they de-platform truth-tellers. Don't rely on anything on Wikipedia – and certainly don't ever give them money.

Third, remember that the collaborators are the enemy. Talk to them and try to explain the truth to them.

Fourth, if you have debts try to pay them off. Don't take on new debts that you wouldn't be able to afford if interest rates soared.

Fifth, insist on paying cash as often as you can. If a shop won't take cash – walk out until you find somewhere that will take cash. Look at awakenedpages.co.uk for shops and businesses to support. Look at the astandinthepark.org website for details of how to meet like-minded people. Subscribe to the thelightpaper.co.uk to keep in touch. Become a distributor for them.

Sixth, visit newspaper websites and share the truth in the comments section. If you see the BBC or any other broadcaster being prejudiced make a formal complaint. Make complaints about newspapers which bend the truth. Report doctors who lie – complain about them to the GMC.

Seventh, prepare for fuel and food shortages. Prepare for price rises in every aspect of your life. Stock up with any medicines you need. Learn first aid. And learn as much as you can about home remedies. Don't use a smart phone. Get a cheap calls-only phone. Don't ever download one of their apps onto any phone or computer. Without apps they can't control us.

Remember: we are living in a world where our own governments have declared war on us.

And most people haven't even noticed.

Freedom, justice, democracy and free speech have all been killed by politicians and compliant mainstream media organisations.

We need to remain constantly aware and suspicious, for eternal paranoia is the price of freedom. A free man must honour truth, integrity, self-respect and dignity – even if in so doing he destroys himself.

Finally, although it may feel like it at times, please remember that you are not alone. More and more people are waking up and once they are awake they don't go back to sleep. We are already a far bigger force than the conspirators would have you believe.

If we are going to win this war then we have to fight hard and with determination and passion and the truth.

Distrust the government, avoid mass media and fight the lies.

And, remember, we have God on our side.

Appendix
The Author's Travails

I've been getting into trouble for years. I didn't want to get into trouble. And I didn't mean to get into trouble. But that's the way it's always been.

In 1964, at the age of 18, I went to Kirkby, Liverpool to spend a year as a Community Service Volunteer.

I arrived as a schoolboy, in a school blazer, tie and flannels. I spent my time there helping old people and working with an army of teenage school-children. I organised groups of teenagers to tidy gardens, paint flats and do shopping for lonely, housebound people.

Nine months later I had seen more of life than I'd seen in the previous 18 years. I had become a professional rebel – fighting for freedom and human rights and against injustices of all kinds.

When I started medical school I carried on working with 'lost' teenagers in Birmingham. I recruited a couple of gangs and got the members to help me run a night-club in the city centre so that kids had somewhere to go in the evenings.

And I spent much of the 1960s and 1970s writing articles and columns which were critical of the establishment.

To begin with, the establishment was moderately tolerant.

My early books such as 'The Medicine Men' and 'Paper Doctors', (both published in the 1970s) were widely praised in the national press. The Guardian newspaper bought serial rights for the first and published a huge extract. The BBC made a programme about it.

During the 1970s and early 1980s, while working as a GP in an English provincial town, I worked a good deal for both broadsheet and tabloid newspapers and for national TV stations. I wrote numerous columns and made several thousand TV and radio programmes. And I wrote a host of books which were mostly very well received and reviewed – appearing in the best-seller lists around the world. I was sued and served with injunctions and so on but probably no more than most authors.

My medical career came to an end in the 1980s when I was fined by the NHS because I refused to put diagnoses on sick notes. I felt that maintaining patient confidentiality was important. I resigned as a GP, though my protest resulted in a change in the regulations.

But then, at the end of the 1980s, there was a not very subtle change in the way the establishment treated original thinking: anyone who questioned the 'official' line was either actively suppressed or attacked. Any questioning of vaccination or vivisection, for example, drew violent attacks from the medical establishment and, in particular, from the pharmaceutical industry.

I was sued by all sorts of people, including a police force. (And I sued one back.) Most of the lawsuits were, I suspect, more to cause annoyance and waste my time. Because of my opposition to vivisection, I had MI5 and private detectives (hired by drug companies) chasing me and tracking me down. My mail was opened and two separate insiders told me that Special Branch had a growing file about me. I was 'door stepped' by journalists on more occasions than I like to remember. I was regularly filmed by police forces. I received writs so thick that they wouldn't fit through the letter box and had to be pushed through a cat flap. I've had papers relating to drug companies stolen from my home. And, of course, my phone has been tapped for years. (I thought it rather comical when a former head of MI6 complained that the Russians had been reading his personal emails. MI5 admitted years ago that they'd been tapping my phone and emails.)

Overnight, I was banned in China where the Chinese Government was so annoyed by a weekly column I wrote for a big Chinese newspaper that they banned all my books in Chinese and also banned other 'foreign' authors. (I was a bestselling author in China and wrote a weekly column for a Chinese newspaper). The column which caused the fuss was one in which I criticised vaccination.

In the UK I was banned from speaking to NHS staff because it was felt that I would be a threat to the pharmaceutical industry. I had been booked to speak about drug side effects at a large conference but I was replaced by a drug company representative and the conference was altered to put the blame for drug side effects onto patients rather than doctors or drug companies.

I resigned from my last national newspaper column in 2003 after the editor refused to publish an article I had written criticising the

Iraq war.

A serious death threat was investigated for many months by the police and by Interpol, and when I travelled to South Africa to speak against vivisection, I was met by an agent of BOSS within hours of arriving in Johannesburg. (He wasn't terribly good at it. He turned up in a silk suit claiming to be an anti-vivisection activist and wanted to know everything about 'my friend ALF'. He didn't realise ALF was an organisation not a person.)

After I exposed the way the AIDS 'crisis' had been exaggerated, I found that I was no longer invited to contribute to TV or radio programmes. And publishers around the world suddenly let my books go out of print or remaindered them – and refused to consider new titles. A German publisher had been selling large amounts of my books but my books disappeared overnight. The publishers did not respond when I asked for royalty statements. That cost me around £30,000 a year in royalties – and a lot of readers in Germany. Much the same sort of thing happened around the world.

Book contracts were suddenly withdrawn and TV companies cancelled invitations. Publishers suddenly decided that they didn't want books they'd been keen to buy. By the late 1990s, for no discernible reason, nasty articles about me started to appear in the national press. A nasty and inaccurate piece about me appeared in The Spectator. It was commissioned by Boris Johnson and written by his sister. (The Spectator had to publish a letter of correction.)

And then came the events of 2020.

In February and March of 2020, I questioned the claim that we were at the start of a major plague. My comments (all of which were entirely accurate and based on fact) proved deeply unpopular with the medical and political establishment. Overnight, without any evidence, I became a conspiracy theorist, a discredited doctor and a danger to mankind.

Twenty years previously, I'd been allotted a Wikipedia page (though I had frequently asked for it to be removed).

Suddenly the content of the page was dramatically changed with no reference to me and no respect for the facts.

All details of my books, TV series and columns were removed and replaced with lies and nonsense.

Wikipedia pages which had been put up about two of my book series (Mrs Caldicot and Bilbury) mysteriously disappeared. Google, which has a 'relationship' with Wikipedia, repeated the lies. It was clear this was all designed to make sure that no one took any notice of what I had to say. It was pretty clearly also designed to destroy me personally and to wreck my book sales. (One or two people have, I think, tried to restore sense to the pages. No one has succeeded because it appears to be mysteriously 'locked'.)

Even the Wikipedia site relating to the award winning movie of my novel Mrs Caldicot's Cabbage War has been deliberately wrecked. The film had terrific reviews, is regularly shown on TV and has over 1,000 reviews at nearly 5 stars on Amazon but Wikipedia now shows only a one star review from the BBC. My name has been removed from the summary box so that I'm not included on other derivative sites and the only time I'm mentioned as the author, I'm described, inevitably, as a conspiracy theorist.

In my view, Wikipedia is a disinformation site, spreading misinformation and defending the indefensible. Wikipedia editors will remove the lies from a page if you give them money. Then when it gets changed back they want more money to tidy it up again. I'm sure that sort of behaviour used to be against the law. At least one of the editors named as responsible for altering my Wikipedia page has, according to Larry Sanger (Wikipedia's co-founder), suspected links to the CIA.

I was accused of spreading misinformation because the truth I was telling was considered inconvenient. I was wrongly accused of having been struck off the medical register. I was even accused of falsely claiming to be a doctor. I was accused of making my videos to 'make money' though I had always refused to monetise them because I didn't want adverts next to my videos. In reality, telling the truth cost me a great deal of money, two years of my life (at a point when time is the one commodity I'm short of), a destroyed reputation, a career in tatters and a constant stream of abuse.

Four decades ago my books were reviewed in most national newspapers and magazines, in countries all around the world. That has changed. My books are now never reviewed or serialised. Publishers in the UK and the US won't publish my books. (I've had four books banned in the last two years. Not even independent platforms will carry them.) It seems quite a price to pay just for telling the truth. None of those who has banned me or attacked me or accused me of spreading misinformation have ever found any inaccuracies in anything I've written. I am widely libelled and sneeringly dismissed, without any evidence whatsoever, as a discredited conspiracy theorist.

Within a few months of starting to make videos for YouTube, I was getting millions of views. I acquired over 200,000 subscribers in record time. Before long, however, YouTube started to take down videos. And then they removed my channel and banned me permanently. They even banned me from looking at other people's videos. Nothing in the videos I made was factually inaccurate. But YouTube doesn't seem to care about freedom or truth. The editors didn't seem to understand what they were doing. Early on I suggested that lockdown victims should take vitamin D supplements. YouTube censored, removed and banned the video. A month or so later the Government issued exactly the same warning.

I then put my videos on a platform called Brand New Tube. Within a short time the platform was told it would be shut down if they continued to host my videos. Bravely, Muhammad Butt, who runs BNT, took the platform base abroad so that I could keep making videos.

I was refused permission to open a Facebook account or a Twitter account. My account on LinkedIn was suddenly closed without warning or explanation. I am not allowed any access to social media sites but fake sites have appeared in my name and are allowed to remain.

My website had been hacked and attacked for decades but things got worse. For two years there have been at least 5,000 to 6,000 hacking attempts every month on the two main sites. Occasionally, the websites have been taken down. My sites have been repeatedly ghosted and hidden (particularly by Google). In particular, I have been hacked by the Americans (including at least two of the various alphabet soup organisations), the Russians and the South Koreans.

During the last two years, half a century of hard work and campaigning has been trashed and my reputation has been steadily destroyed by lies and libels on the internet and in the mainstream media. I was banned by all mainstream media, and TV and radio stations attacked me without giving me a right to reply. One national newspaper in the UK claimed that I was pretending to be a doctor. I have, inevitably, been threatened with legal action and I've received death threats.

Privately and professionally, sharing the truth in 2020 was the worst thing I ever did. It has brought me and my beloved, hard-working and constantly loyal wife nothing but personal and professional pain. It has taken up nearly every minute of my life for two years.

The aim of the attacks was not, simply to destroy me – it was to stop people listening to anything I said, or reading anything I wrote. Before March 2020 I had many millions of readers around the world. I wonder how many I have left now. Precious few, I suspect. How do people know or care that the word 'discredited', plucked out of thin air and applied to my name by an unreliable encyclopaedia called Wikipedia, widely spread by that evil search engine Google, is just a libel and not a fact?

And this sort of defamation doesn't just break and silence the individuals who are targeted – it also dissuades others from speaking out.

I was expelled from the Royal Society of Arts because 'of my views and my recent involvement in the BBC panorama programme'. That's what they said. This seemed to me to be a bit like arresting someone because they'd been mugged. I was never invited to appear on the programme they mentioned. (The BBC boasts that it won't ever give airtime to those questioning vaccination 'whether they're right or wrong'.)

The abuse on social media grew and grew. It isn't normal, unpleasant social media abuse. It is a campaign of suppression and oppression, decorated with malicious lies, invented and spread to cause doubt and to help keep the truth suppressed. The ruthlessness and cruelty and refusal to debate are evidence of the fundamental wickedness. (I've frequently offered to debate with 'the other side' but all my challenges have been ignored.)

If my videos or articles are put on sites such as YouTube by other people they are taken down within minutes. Many people admit that they won't put my videos on their Twitter or Facebook channels lest they be punished. On one occasion when I was invited to speak in public in 2021, the organiser had four venues cancelled.

Someone watches everything I do. In May 2022, a publisher working outside the UK and the US finally produced an English language paperback version of my thrice banned book 'Covid-19: The Greatest Hoax in History'. I mentioned the book's publication on my website. Within hours the publisher's PayPal account was closed making it difficult for him to sell books by mail order. He then opened another payment account with a different company and, almost immediately, that account was also closed.

And on it goes. There is much more but I expect you are as bored with reading this sorry tale as I am of writing it.

Everything I've written was absolutely accurate and time and time again my predictions have been correct. In reality it hasn't been difficult to work out what would happen next. (The videos I've made for BNT are still available there and on BitChute and other sites and the transcripts of my YouTube videos are available in books and on my websites.)

I tell you all this to show just how bad things have become, how the truth is suppressed and how truth-tellers are mercilessly and ruthlessly demonised.

My accusers and detractors will never debate with me. They are not interested in the truth – only in propaganda.

Finally…

If you found this book helpful, I would be enormously grateful if you would write a suitable review.

Printed in Great Britain
by Amazon